EAT
NYC

EAT NYC

Yasmin
Enjoy!
Newman

Photography by Alan Benson

Smith
Street
Books

Iconic Recipes that Feed the City

To Terry and Krista—
for NYC

"New York, my dear New York."

Contents

"COME EARLY, STAY LATE"

Author's Note
11

TRY OUR ALL-DAY MENU!

Morning

BREAKFAST + BRUNCH
20

Contents Eat NYC

"COME EARLY, STAY LATE"

Noon

LUNCH + STREET EATS
88

Night

DINNER + MIDNIGHT SNACKS
158

AUTHOR'S NOTE

◆◆◆

I'm not a New Yorker, but I've had the great fortune to experience New York. Over the years, I've spent short and long periods of time in the city, living through its different seasons. This is my second book on New York and, as an Australian, writing each one has been exhilarating—and daunting.

Thankfully, I've had the luck to see it through multiple lenses: my own eyes as an enamored visitor and a seasoned food and travel writer; my brother's, an expat who came for the New York dream 10 years ago and like many before him never returned home; and my sister-in-law, born in New Jersey a ferry ride away, and a New Yorker for over two decades—along with their friends and family from different walks of life.

For me, the best way to discover a city is always through its food, venturing away from its landmarks to alleyways and corners where everyday life takes place. Nowhere is this more true than in New York, whose rich tapestry of communal gardens, basketball courts, and mural-adorned walls can be experienced with each passing street. In the countless meals I've savored here researching my books, I've only experienced a fraction of this city, where every square foot reveals something new, and the scene is always evolving.

Each time I return, I'm swept up in never-ending discovery and unapologetic authenticity, from high to low and everything in between. I'm not the first and certainly not the last to feel the pull of New York, a city that casts its spell on us all.

THE FIVE BOROUGHS

I
MANHATTAN

II
THE BRONX

III
QUEENS

IV
BROOKLYN

V
STATEN ISLAND

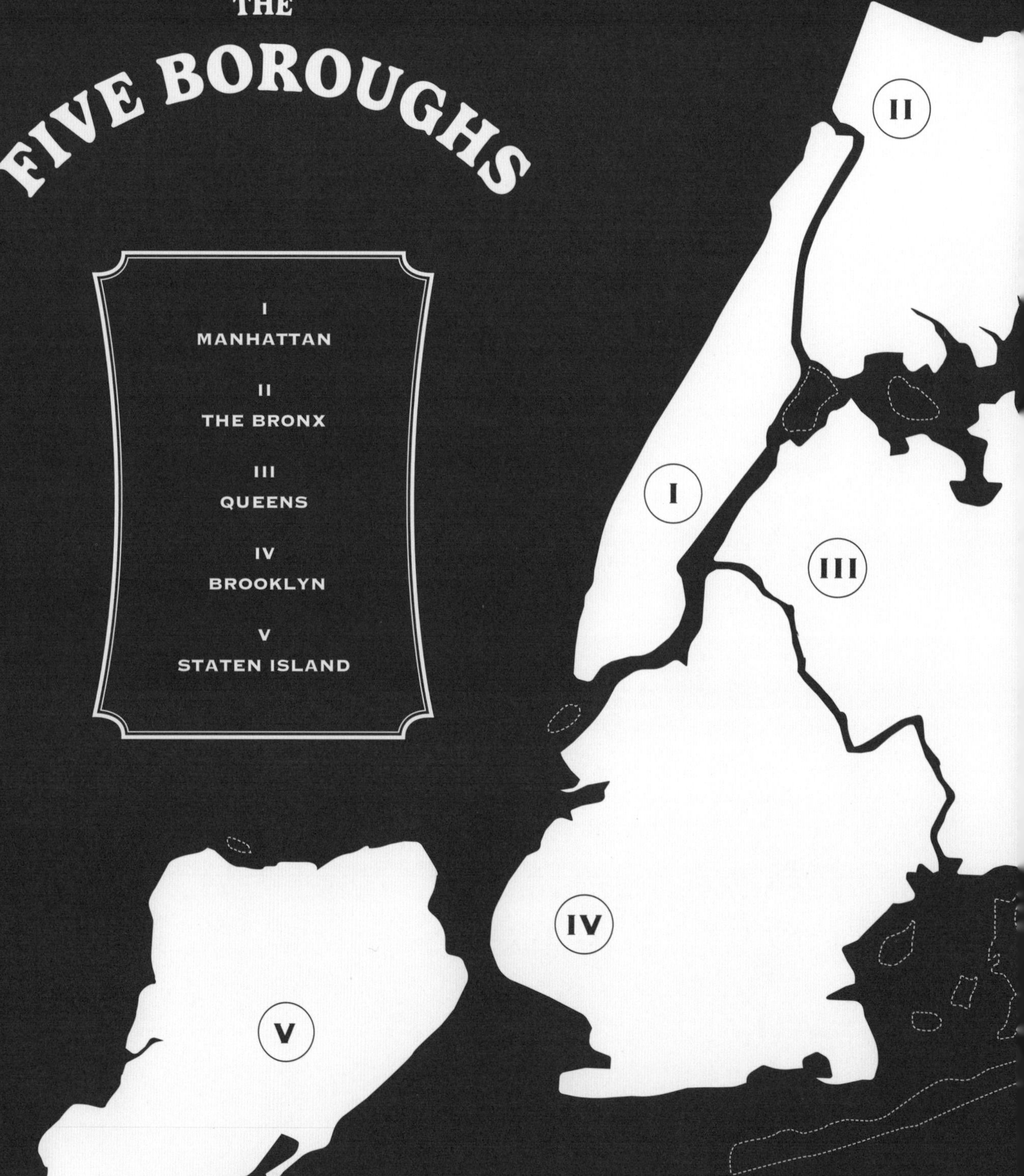

A FEW NEIGHBORHOODS TO START EXPLORING

Manhattan

Tribeca
SoHo
West Village
Chelsea
Chinatown
Lower East Side
Nolita
East Village
Union Square + Flatiron
Murray Hill
Midtown
Upper West Side
Upper East Side
Harlem

Brooklyn

Williamsburg
Greenpoint
Red Hook
Park Slope + Prospect Heights
Bed–Stuy
Bushwick
Carroll Gardens + Cobble Hill

Queens

Astoria
Flushing
Jackson Heights
Ridgewood

INTRODUCTION

◆◆◆

Welcome to the bright lights and the five boroughs of New York City. Cross an avenue or street and there's a new neighborhood—and dish—to discover. The vast grid of the city is a smorgasbord brought to life, where eating a deli sandwich is as superlative as dining at a fine restaurant. From street food to hot spots, and almost every cuisine and food fixation in between, there's something for everyone in NYC—and more of it than any other place in the world.

Of the world's cities, New York is one people feel they know, even if they've never been here. From Broadway to Wall Street, the birth of hip hop in the Bronx and the blossoming of Beat literature in Greenwich Village, the "I'll have what she's having," and I ♥ NY, New York has long been a muse for books and films, and helped shape global culture.

The same goes for its food. Bagels and pizza by the slice, Katz's Delicatessen and Magnolia Bakery—the city's iconic dishes and venues are household names, and innovations from waldorf salad to cronuts have spread throughout the world.

What makes the Big Apple such an incubator of inspiration and experience? Partly, its sheer size. Home to more than eight million people, New York City is the most densely populated city in the United States—its numbers swelling with tourists from all corners of the globe. With more than 25,000 restaurants, there's enough critical mass to cater to any niche.

Then there is its unparalleled diversity. There are more immigrants in New York than ever before—roughly 3.1 million at last count, hailing from more than 180 countries. Around 200 distinct cuisines now call the Big Apple home, from Ukrainian to Hunanese, Ecuadorian, and Nigerian.

Here, difference is a celebrated cornerstone and you can travel the world simply by eating. At the same time, New York makes everything its own. Jewish American delis, Italian-American restaurants and halal carts blending South Asian, Middle Eastern, Mediterranean and Caribbean cuisines are just a few of the distinct culinary cultures born from all social walks living side by side.

Continued

→

New York's fascination with food is also rooted in city living. With notoriously small apartments, dining is a relished moment to step out. Coffee shops, neighborhood bars, and sidewalk restaurants offer a place to come together with friends or strike up a conversation with strangers—simply walk around the corner, or jump on a subway a few stops away.

From a bird's eye view, New York is a bustling metropolis. Zoom in and it's a mosaic of character-filled communities. From the historic brownstones of West Village and cobbled streets of SoHo, the storied grit of Chinatown and Lower East Side, the melting pot of Astoria and Harlem, the grandeur of the Upper East and West Sides, and cool mod-industrial Tribeca and Chelsea, the journey in NYC is just as good as the destination, seeing the streets and culinary options change shape with each passing corner.

Each season also brings new life, or a return to cherished experiences. Park picnics and cold, creamy desserts in summer. Gulping bowls of ramen and cider in fall. Cozy upstate getaways and grilled cheese and tomato soup specials come winter—and spring, blossoming with new produce from farmers' markets.

In a city this big (and a book this small), it's impossible to share it all. A lifetime is not enough to even see it all, but this book hopes to give you a taste of the city and the joys of morning, noon and night marked in meals. The recipes are inspired by favorite renditions in the city today, or amalgams of the countless versions made over the years and centuries. Likewise, their origins combine various accounts, with multiple claims of invention or hearsay twisting into truths over time—the mystery, in part, adding to their allure.

From a bacon, egg, and cheese for breakfast at a Greenpoint bodega, lunch at an old-world steakhouse, and sunset drinks on a Williamsburg rooftop, to pasta alla vodka at a new West Village hotspot, Egyptian at a local haunt in Astoria, and smash burgers in East Village come 2 am, each day in New York is varied, vibrant and new. Through a handful of neighborhoods from Manhattan, Brooklyn and Queens and 50 quintessential dishes, this book is an homage to the city's many enclaves and cuisines. EAT NYC.

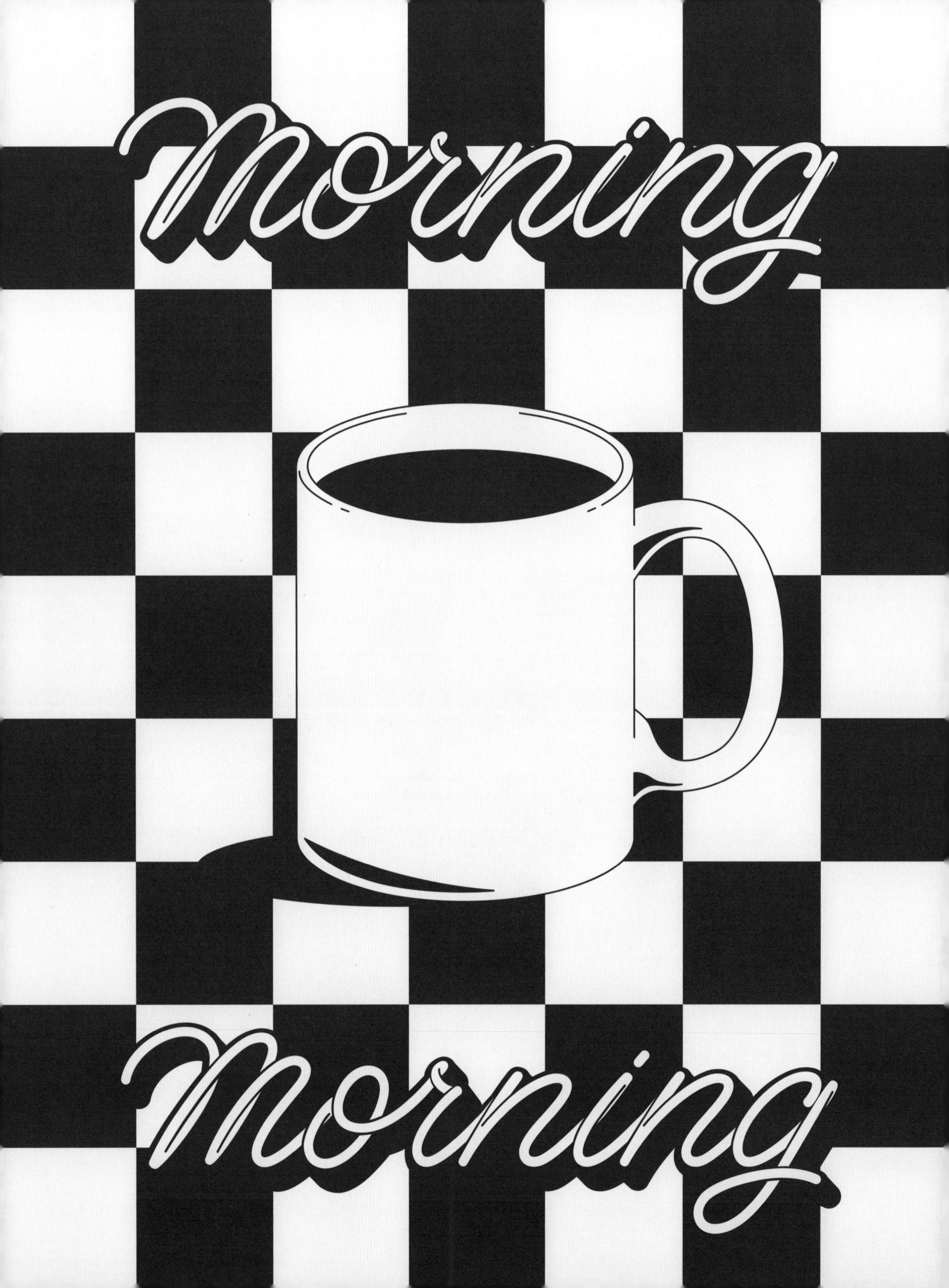
Morning
Morning

MORNING

◆◆◆

In a city that's late to end, it's no surprise it's later to start, at least in some neighborhoods. Once it has shaken off the night before and prepped for the hustle of the day to come, it's all systems go.

For busy New Yorkers, weekday breakfast is often on the move, which explains the quick and energizing picks of choice—gulps of iced coffee and warm cups of joe, fresh bagels schmeared with cream cheese, and steaming hot breakfast sandwiches. Just don't confuse speed with lack of quality and craftsmanship; coffee shops, neighborhood bagel spots, old-school delis, and even bodegas turn out a top-notch selection. Join the queue and order loudly.

There's also the call of perfect breakfast pastries and sweet snacks: pillowy glazed donuts, concentric-shaped crullers, sticky buns and frosted cinnamon rolls, softball-size chocolate chip cookies, and flaky pastries in seasonal flavors. You can find them in the big-name bakeries as well as light-filled cafes doubling as workspaces for small apartment–confined locals.

Finally, it's the weekend. In a sleepless city, a sleep-in is in order, followed by brunch. At times, streets in West Village to Williamsburg close off and pedestrians, bike riders, and stalls take over. The most important meal on Saturdays and Sundays, brunch starts any time from 11 am to 2 pm and usually runs for hours. There's the dim sum route in Chinatown or Flushing, with bustling rooms and carts laden with delicacies. Or settle in for spicy bloody Marys and bubbly mimosas, endless coffee refills, stacks of pancakes or French toast and eggs every which way at neighborhood restaurants. From classic to inventive, brunch is infused with global influences reflective of Gotham's population, and paired with atmospheric spaces for lingering with friends.

Here are how days start (and taste) in New York—and they've only just begun.

Everything bagels

MAKES
8

Bagels arrived in New York with Polish immigrants in the late 19th century—first peddled in street carts on the Lower East Side within the Jewish community, then eventually becoming a beacon of Jewish culture in its new home. Today it's the ultimate New York breakfast bread and known the world over.

The bagel's signature crust and chewy texture come from boiling the dough rings briefly in a water bath (traditionally with lye or malt extract, but dark brown sugar is subbed here for ease), before baking in the oven. Some locals say its trademark flavor comes from New York City water—one reason why it's rare to find a true copy anywhere else.

The "everything bagel"—coated in salt, dried onion, dried garlic, poppy seeds and sesame seeds (a combination of all the singular classics)—first appeared in the 1970s, and is now synonymous with New York, too.

10 fl oz (300 ml) lukewarm water
2 teaspoons dried yeast
3⅓ cups (500 g) bread flour
2 teaspoons fine sea salt
1 tablespoon dark brown sugar, plus 2 tablespoons extra for boiling
"Everything bagel" mix, or sesame seeds or poppy seeds and sea salt flakes, for scattering

Place the water and yeast in the bowl of a stand mixer fitted with a dough hook and leave for 5 minutes, or until frothy. Add the flour, salt, and sugar and knead for 10 minutes to develop the protein in the dough; it will be smooth and elastic. Transfer to a lightly greased bowl, cover and set aside in a warm place for 1 hour, or until risen about one and a half times in size.

Line two baking trays with baking paper. Divide the dough into eight even pieces, then roll each piece into a smooth ball. Divide the balls among the baking trays, cover with greased plastic wrap and rest for 30 minutes, or until slightly risen.

Preheat the oven to 430°F (220°C). Half-fill a large saucepan with water, add the extra sugar and bring to the boil.

Using your finger, poke a hole through the center of each dough ball, then twirl the dough on your finger to stretch the hole until it's 1½–2 in (4–5 cm) in diameter.

Working in batches, carefully transfer two or three bagels to the boiling water. (To make transferring easier, cut the baking paper into squares around the bagels, then remove the paper from the water with tongs.) Boil for 2 minutes, then flip the bagels over and cook for a further 1 minute. Remove the bagels from the water and return to the tray. Scatter with some of the seed mix. Repeat with the remaining bagels.

Bake the bagels for 20–25 minutes, until golden, then cool completely on a wire rack. For classic ways to enjoy your bagels, see the serving ideas on page 30.

Classic Bagel

SANDWICHES

ORDER HERE

FRESH TODAY

LOX!

CREAM CHEESE, WITH VINE-RIPENED TOMATOES, RED ONION & CAPERS

$15.99 + TAX

B.E.C.

BACON, SCRAMBLED EGG, AMERICAN CHEESE + $13.99

YOU'VE GOTTA TRY

HOT SAUCE + TAX

YUM EGG SALAD WITH

BUTTER LETTUCE & RED ONION

$11.99 + TAX

PIZZA

FRESH MOZZARELLA, MARINARA SAUCE AND BASIL

$13.99 + TAX

TURKEY CLUB

TURKEY, BACON, VINE-RIPENED TOMATO, LETTUCE WITH RUSSIAN DRESSING

$14.99 + TAX

TUNA MELT

TUNA SALAD, MELTED SWISS CHEESE

$13.99 + TAX

Bagel schmears

MAKES 3 × 10½ OZ (300 G) SCHMEARS

How do you eat a bagel in New York? According to locals, the first step is choosing the type: plain, salt, sesame, poppy seed, onion, garlic or everything. Next, untoasted or toasted. If it's fresh—and the best bagels are consumed within five hours of baking and, ideally, still warm—you don't need to toast. Finally, the topping. Following Jewish kosher tradition, dairy and meat can't be combined, which gave rise to the classics: simply butter, cream cheese "schmear" (Yiddish for "spread"), and cream cheese with "lox" (Yiddish for "salmon"). Today, you can choose between beloved sandwich fillings and a range of schmears.

Scallion & dill cream cheese

9 oz (250 g) cream cheese, softened

1 tablespoon milk

3 scallions (spring onions), white and green parts thinly sliced, plus extra to serve

small handful of chopped dill, plus extra to serve (optional)

Honey chipotle cream cheese

9 oz (250 g) cream cheese, softened

2 tablespoons pureed chipotle in adobo sauce

1 tablespoon honey

Caramelized shallot & garlic butter

1½ tablespoons olive oil

4 Asian shallots, finely chopped

3 garlic cloves, finely chopped

1 teaspoon sugar

9 oz (250 g) salted butter, chopped, softened

To make the scallion and dill cream cheese schmear, place the cream cheese and milk in the bowl of a stand mixer and beat until light and smooth. Add the scallion and dill. Season with salt and pepper and beat until well combined. Transfer to a small bowl and scatter with extra scallion and dill, if desired.

To make the honey chipotle cream cheese, place the cream cheese in the bowl of a stand mixer and beat until light and smooth. Add the chipotle and honey, season with salt and pepper, and beat until well combined. Transfer to a small bowl to serve.

To make the caramelized shallot and garlic butter, heat the olive oil in a frying pan over medium heat. Cook the shallot, stirring, for 4 minutes, or until softened. Add the garlic, season with salt and pepper and cook for 1 minute, or until fragrant. Reduce the heat to medium–low, sprinkle the sugar over and cook for a further 5 minutes, or until the shallot and garlic are caramelized. Remove the mixture from the pan and allow to cool completely. Place the butter in the bowl of a stand mixer and beat until light and fluffy. Add the caramelized onion mixture and beat until well combined. Transfer to a small bowl.

Now, simply split a bagel and spread generously with your chosen schmear.

165 Avenue A, New York,
NY 10009

NYC's
Number 1
Street Food

Christopher Pugliese

I was born in Brooklyn. I'm 53 years old now and I've lived in New York my whole life. I love it sometimes so much it hurts. I've traveled and seen lots of places, but there's something very special about New York City.

Gravesend in Brooklyn was sort of a landing place for immigrants who'd come to New York City, and there are a lot of Italian Americans and Jewish Americans concentrated in one area. I spent a lot of time in Coney Island and Brighton Beach, but once I got old enough to take the subway, I'd cut school and run around East Village looking for Keith Haring art and watching guys juggling swords and eating fire, and playing music in Washington Square Park.

I got my first real job working for a restaurant in the West Village and fell head over heels for the restaurant business. Being a kid from Brooklyn, where everyone was pretty much the same, to come into the city

and work with people from all over the world, all different cultures, and all different backgrounds, was the greatest thing that could ever have happened to me.

I never ever, ever thought I would open a bagel store. I worked in bagel shops as a kid. It was hard work. It was dirty work. I had horrible bosses that I hated back then. But being hard on me gave me a great work ethic. When I met my wife, she was always having me bring back bagels from Brooklyn. And it dawned on me there was not one bagel shop from Avenue D to Broadway. It might be kind of hard to picture right now, but at the time the bagel industry was kind of dead. No one had opened a bagel shop in a long time, and most were just dives.

I walked the avenues of New York City studying every bagel shop and took all my restaurant knowledge and put it into Tompkins. In 2011, we opened on Avenue A at 165 Avenue A. It was like a dream to me to be by Tompkins

Square Park and in the heart of the East Village where I used to run around as a kid. Sometimes still, I walk down the block and I'm like, how is this? How do I have a store here?

We have a big open kitchen where we make every single thing that we sell. We don't cut corners, so I guess we'd be considered slow food. When I opened, other places were serving premade egg sandwiches and popping them in convection ovens. They weren't making a deli sandwich to order. And now I think it's pretty much the standard.

From day one, we had a massive line. I had no idea how seriously New Yorkers take their bagels. I got my ass kicked for the first few years because we were so busy, but when we made more money, I was able to get more help.

For New York City, I think bagels are the number one street food—they're so diverse. You can make a breakfast sandwich or deli sandwich, simply spread on some butter or cream cheese, or eat it plain. You can add whatever you want, and I think people like that. We have a lot of second- and third-generation New Yorkers for whom the bagel has a history. It ties the generations together.

Sesame ═ BAGEL

WEEKLY SPECIAL

CREAM CHEESE FLAVORS

PLAIN $4.95	LOX SPREAD $7.95	WALNUT RAISIN $5.95
LIGHT $4.95	OLIVE –PIMENTO $5.95	STRAWBERRY $6.95
SCALLION $5.95	CUCUMBER DILL $5.95	ESPRESSO $5.95
VEGGIE $5.95	WASABI $5.95	FIG & HONEY $6.95

SPECIALTY

PEPPERS, MOZZARELLA, ONIONS 10.00
LETTUCE, ONIONS 10.00

SS, BACON, LETTUCE, ONION, TOMATO
AR. ONIONS, ROASTED PEPPERS 10.00

TOMATO, BASIL 8.50
LA, PESTO, BALSAMIC VIN. 10.00

ONIONS 19.50

B.E.C.
(Bacon, Egg, & Cheese)

MAKES
2

For New Yorkers, bacon, egg, and cheese is the quintessential breakfast sandwich. It's the combo that always hits the spot: simple, reliable, and unsurpassed. It's available at every corner bodega in every part of the city, and any breakfast menu you come across, too. (It's colloquially known as B.E.C.—which you'll hear yelled out in morning breakfast queues.)

There are a few options—scrambled or over-easy eggs, thick-cut or crispy bacon, added hot sauce and ketchup, even bagels in place of the traditional plain or kaiser poppy seed roll. Then there's the cheese, melted onto and rippled through the eggs as they're cooked and folded, and lightly toasted bread, so it's more warm than crisp. Wrap in deli paper sheets, then slice in half to go.

7 oz (200 g) streaky bacon
2 kaiser poppy seed rolls or bagels, split
1½ oz (40 g) butter
4 eggs
4 slices American cheese
hot sauce and ketchup, for drizzling

Place the bacon slices in a large cold frying pan over medium heat. Fry, pressing occasionally to flatten and crisp the slices, for 4 minutes, or until the fat has rendered and the bacon is starting to crisp. Turn the bacon over and cook for a further 2 minutes, or until crisp. Remove from the pan and cover to keep warm.

Toast one of the rolls in a toaster until lightly toasted (you don't want it crisp). Spread with ⅓ oz (10 g) of the butter. Place the base of the toasted roll on a large sheet of baking paper or foil.

Melt ⅓ oz (10 g) of the remaining butter in a frying pan over medium heat. Crack two eggs into a small bowl, season with salt and pepper and whisk until just combined (you want some egg whites still visible). Cook in the pan for 30 seconds then, using a spatula, pull the egg toward the center and tilt the pan so the egg runs to the empty part of the pan. Keep repeating until the egg is almost set but still a little runny. Top with two cheese slices and cover the pan with a lid. Cook for 30 seconds to melt the cheese slightly, then top with half the bacon. Fold over the egg so the bacon is in the middle—then fold in half again, if you can, so it's roughly the size of the roll.

Using the spatula, slide the mixture onto the buttered roll base. Drizzle with hot sauce and ketchup to taste, then sandwich with the roll top. Wrap in the paper or foil and stand for at least 3 minutes, for the steam to soften the bread and the cheese to melt.

Repeat with the remaining ingredients to make a second sandwich. Cut the sandwiches in half and serve.

Burnt butter pecan donuts

MAKES
8

Donuts have been an essential part of New York's culture since 1673, when the first donut shop in the country opened in the city. The various delectable styles available today trace the fascinating history of immigration and innovation, from old-fashioned sour cream rounds and light choux crullers to delicate cake donuts and crisp flaky cronuts. At dedicated donut purveyors and diners, there's usually a selection of yeasted donuts, generously sized and glazed in classic honey dip or seasonal flavors, like these burnt butter pecan donuts. There are few things more satisfying than biting into the soft pillowy embrace of a freshly fried ring.

⅔ cup (160 ml) lukewarm milk
1 teaspoon dried yeast
2 cups (300 g) all-purpose (plain) flour, plus extra if needed and for dusting
1½ tablespoons superfine (caster) sugar
1 egg
2 oz (60 g) unsalted butter, melted and cooled
½ teaspoon fine sea salt
vegetable oil, for deep-frying

Burnt butter pecan glaze

3½ oz (100 g) unsalted butter, chopped
2½ cups (315 g) confectioners' (icing) sugar, sifted
¼ cup (60 ml) milk, plus extra if needed
3½ oz (100 g) pecans, toasted and finely chopped

Put the milk and yeast in the bowl of a stand mixer attached with the dough hook and leave for 5 minutes, or until frothy.

Add the flour, sugar, egg, butter, and salt and mix on low speed until the mixture comes together. Increase the speed to high and knead for 5 minutes, or until smooth. The dough will be quite soft; add 1–2 tablespoons more flour if necessary.

Transfer to a greased bowl, then cover and set aside at room temperature for 1 hour, or until doubled in size.

On a lightly floured work surface, roll the dough out to ½ in (1.5 cm) thick. Cut out donuts with a floured donut cutter, or a pair of 3¼ in (8 cm) and 1¼ in (3 cm) cookie cutters. Gently knead the scraps, taking care not to overwork the dough, then repeat to make more donuts.

Arrange the donuts on two baking trays lined with baking paper. Cover with greased plastic wrap or kitchen towel and set aside in a warm place for 45 minutes, or until slightly risen and puffed. If your kitchen is cool, simply warm your oven to 400°F (200°C), then turn off the heat and prove the dough inside, with the door ajar.

Continued

To make the burnt butter glaze, warm the butter in a small saucepan over medium heat and cook for 5 minutes, or until nutty and fragrant. Transfer to a bowl. Add the confectioners' sugar and stir until combined. Stir in the milk until you have a smooth glazing consistency; it shouldn't be too thick or too thin. Add another 2 teaspoons of milk if necessary.

Before the donuts have finished rising, fill a large saucepan one-third full with vegetable oil and heat over medium heat to 350°F (180°C).

Carefully transfer two or three donuts to the hot oil. Cook for 45–60 seconds, until golden. Flip them over with a spatula and cook for a further 45–60 seconds, until golden all over. Transfer to a wire rack lined with paper towel and repeat with the remaining donuts. Make sure the oil returns to 350°F (180°C) between frying.

While the donuts are still warm, dunk them in the glaze and turn to coat all over, then transfer to a wire rack set over a tray to catch the drips. (If the glaze has stiffened, gently warm in the microwave in 10-second bursts.) Scatter with the toasted pecans.

Set the donuts aside to firm for 10 minutes, then eat warm or fresh the same day.

Honey Dip

White Cream Coconut

Sugar Jelly

Eggs your way with home fries

SERVES
2-4

Home fries are classic Americana and a New York diner favorite, sitting on menus as a side offering to breakfast eggs or lunch sandwiches. A good home fry is an addictive mix of crunchy-crispy crust with a soft and tender center, achieved by boiling and then frying in oil—all in one pan. Finish with simple salt flakes, or with vinegar for a twist, and serve with eggs your way, and toast.

1 lb 2 oz (500 g) unpeeled
  floury potatoes, cut into
  ½ in (1.5 cm) chunks
⅓ cup (80 ml) olive oil
1 onion, chopped
2 teaspoons red wine vinegar
  (optional)
2 oz (60 g) butter
4 eggs
toast, to serve (optional)

Put the potato in a single layer in a large frying pan over high heat. Add ½ cup (125 ml) of water, cover with a lid and bring to the boil. Reduce the heat to medium and cook, covered, for 8 minutes, or until the water has evaporated; the potatoes should be tender but firm.

Drizzle 2 tablespoons of the oil over the potato and season with salt. Gently toss to combine, scraping up any skin stuck to the pan (try to keep the chunks intact, but don't worry if the potato breaks up a little). Increase the heat to medium–high and cook, without stirring, for 7 minutes, or until golden and crisp underneath. Turn the potato over, drizzle with another 1 tablespoon of the olive oil and cook for a further 5 minutes, or until golden and crisp (not all sides will be crisp). Remove from the heat.

Meanwhile, heat the remaining olive oil in a separate frying pan over medium heat. Add the onion and cook, stirring, for 5–7 minutes, until soft. Season with salt. Add the onion to the potato, drizzle with the vinegar (if using) and gently toss to combine.

Melt the butter in another large frying pan over medium heat. Crack in the eggs and cook for 3 minutes, or until the yolks are just set.

Divide the home fries among plates and add the fried eggs. Drizzle any remaining butter from the pan over the eggs and serve with toast, if desired.

Bialy

MAKES
8

A puffed round roll with a sweet dimple in the center, bialy hold a special place in the hearts of New Yorkers. Hailing from Bialystock, Poland, the bread rose to prominence in the city along with bagels in the early 20th century, thanks to Polish Jewish bakers, and the two are still often compared for their ring-like looks. The bialy's defining traits are a soft springy crumb and a flour-kissed crust made by rolling on a lightly dusted surface, plus its signature caramelized onion filling—a vestige of a long tradition of Jewish onion breads (said to stretch plain dough into a meal).

This recipe uses an easy overnight poolish (starter) for a delicious depth of flavor. Toast the bialy and spread simply with butter, which melts into the crumb, or schmear with cream cheese—and receive an in-the-know nod from locals.

3⅓ cups (500 g) bread flour, plus extra for dusting
¾ teaspoon dried yeast
1½ cups (375 ml) lukewarm water
2 teaspoons fine sea salt
butter or cream cheese, to serve

Onion & poppy seed filling

2 tablespoons olive oil
1 onion, chopped
1 teaspoon poppy seeds

Place 1⅔ cups (250 g) of the flour in a bowl with ¼ teaspoon of the yeast and 1 cup (250 ml) of the water. Stir until combined, then cover and set aside overnight.

The next morning, your poolish will be bubbly and tripled in volume. Transfer to the bowl of a stand mixer fitted with a dough hook. Add the remaining 1⅔ cups (250 g) of flour, ½ teaspoon of yeast, ½ cup (125 ml) of water and the salt. Knead for 5 minutes, or until well combined. Transfer to a greased bowl, then cover and set aside in a warm place for 1 hour, or until doubled in size.

Turn the dough out onto a floured work surface and divide into eight 3½ oz (100 g) pieces. Shape each piece into a ball. Place on two baking trays lined with baking paper. Cover with greased plastic wrap and set aside for 2 hours, or until puffy.

Meanwhile, to make the onion and poppy seed filling, heat the olive oil in a saucepan over medium heat. Cook the onion, stirring, for 4 minutes, or until softened. Remove from the heat, season with salt and pepper and stir in the poppy seeds.

Preheat the oven to 480°F (250°C), or as high as your oven will go. (If you have a baking stone, preheat it in the oven as well, for a crisper bialy base.)

Shape the dough into bialy by stretching the balls into 4¾ in (12 cm) rounds, and using your thumbs to press down in the center—without going all the way through (think a bagel without a hole). Make sure the center is thin and there is a rim around the edge. Spoon the filling into the center of the bialy.

Bake for 8–10 minutes, until light golden. Transfer to a wire rack to cool slightly. Serve warm with butter or cream cheese.

SMOKED FIS

500 700

600 600 750

No Smoking
or Electronic Cigarette Use

NYC

New York crumb cake

SERVES
12–16

In bakeries, bodegas, and coffee shops, generous slices of crumb cake call out from the counter. The breakfast treat combines a classic coffee cake base with a layer of cinnamon-scented streusel, but the defining New York touch (or New Jersey, depending on who's telling the story) is the ratio, size, and texture of the crumb— at least a third to three-quarters of the cake—and large, fall-apart-in-your-mouth rubbles. With sour cream and dark brown sugar rippled through, it's wonderfully light, rich, and crunchy at the same time, and perfect with your morning coffee. Dust generously with icing sugar for the signature snowy finish.

6½ oz (180 g) unsalted butter, chopped, softened
1½ cups (330 g) superfine (caster) sugar
3 eggs
10½ oz (300 g) sour cream
⅓ cup (80 ml) milk
1 teaspoon natural vanilla extract
2¼ cups (335 g) all-purpose (plain) flour
1 teaspoon baking powder
1 teaspoon baking soda
½ teaspoon fine sea salt
confectioners' (icing) sugar, for dusting

Crumb topping

10 oz (285 g) all-purpose (plain) flour
10½ oz (300 g) dark brown sugar
1½ tablespoons ground cinnamon
½ teaspoon fine sea salt
6½ oz (180 g) unsalted butter, melted

Preheat the oven to 350°F (180°C). Grease a 13 in × 9 in (32.5 cm × 23 cm) baking tin and line with baking paper.

To make the crumb topping, combine the flour, sugar, cinnamon, and salt in a bowl. Pour in the melted butter and stir until well combined. Set aside.

Using a stand mixer or electric beaters, beat the butter and superfine sugar in a large bowl until light and creamy. Add the eggs, one at a time, beating until well combined after each addition. Add the sour cream, milk, and vanilla extract and beat to combine.

Sift the flour, baking powder, baking soda, and salt into a bowl and stir to combine. In batches, add the flour mixture to the liquid ingredients, beating until just combined.

Transfer the batter to the prepared tin and smooth the top.

Using your hands, squeeze small handfuls of the crumb topping to compact it, then crumble into smaller and larger clumps over the batter. Press down gently to lodge the clumps in the batter and cover the top completely.

Bake for 50–60 minutes, until a skewer inserted into the center comes out clean. Leave to cool in the tin, then dust generously with confectioners' sugar. Cut into rectangles to serve.

Chinatown baked pork buns

MAKES
16

During the 1870s, Chinese migrants in New York City began to concentrate around Mott and Mulberry streets, and the heart of Chinatown was born. Now including neighborhoods in Brooklyn and Queens, New York's Chinatown is the largest in the United States. Each regional cuisine and purveyor etched a new specialty in the streets, but a perennial favorite is char siu bao—especially the burnished baked buns at Mei Lai Wah. Crowds mill out the front and snake down the street for these sweet-meets-savory rounds, perfectly sized for eating on the go, or devouring straight away as the hot tender filling spills into your mouth (and perfectly priced, too, at under $2). The key is the dough, which uses a tanzhong (roux), making the dough incredibly soft.

2 tablespoons vegetable oil
1 small onion, finely chopped
1 lb 2 oz (500 g) char siu pork, diced
¼ cup (60 ml) oyster sauce
¼ cup (60 ml) soy sauce
2 tablespoons granulated sugar
1 tablespoon sesame oil
1 tablespoon cornstarch (cornflour), dissolved in 1 tablespoon water
1 egg, lightly whisked

Tanzhong dough

2⅓ cups (350 g) low-protein flour (cake flour), plus an extra 2 tablespoons and a little for dusting
½ cup (110 g) superfine (caster) sugar
2 teaspoons dried yeast
1 teaspoon fine sea salt
½ cup (125 ml) milk
1 egg
2 oz (60 g) unsalted butter, chopped, softened

To make the tanzhong dough, place the extra 2 tablespoons of flour and ½ cup (125 ml) of water in a small saucepan over medium heat. Cook, whisking, for 2 minutes, or until thickened to a paste (tanzhong). Transfer to a bowl to cool.

Place the remaining flour, the sugar, yeast, and salt in the bowl of a stand mixer fitted with a dough hook. Whisk to combine. Add the milk, egg, and tanzhong and knead for 3 minutes, or until the dough comes together. Add the butter, one piece at a time, kneading until combined, then knead for a further 8 minutes, or until the dough is smooth and elastic (it will be quite sticky).

Transfer the dough to a greased bowl, then cover and stand for 1 hour, or until doubled in size. (You can also make the dough ahead of time and refrigerate after it's proved—which also makes it less sticky when rolling.)

To make the filling, heat the vegetable oil in a saucepan over medium heat. Cook the onion, stirring, for 3 minutes, or until softened. Add the pork, oyster sauce, soy sauce, sugar, sesame oil, cornstarch mixture, and ¼ cup (60 ml) of water. Cook, stirring, for 5 minutes, or until the sauce has thickened. Remove from the heat and allow to cool.

Continued

Line two baking trays with baking paper. Turn the dough out onto a lightly floured work surface and divide into 16 even pieces. Roll each piece into a ball, then flatten to a 4 in (10 cm) round, using your fingers to make the rounds thinner at the edges (this ensures an even amount of bread at the top and bottom of the bun).

Place a scant tablespoon of the filling in the center of one dough round, then pull the edges of the dough up and around the filling to enclose, pinching or twisting the dough to seal. Place the bun, seam side down, on one of the prepared trays, then repeat with the remaining dough and filling. Cover the buns with greased plastic wrap and set aside in a warm place for 30 minutes.

Preheat the oven to 350°F (180°C).

Brush the buns with the beaten egg, then transfer one tray to the oven and bake the buns for 15 minutes, or until golden. Transfer to a wire rack to cool, then repeat with the remaining buns. Serve warm, or at room temperature.

Morning

Nutella babka

SERVES
8

Ask a New Yorker to list the city's sweets and babka will undoutedbly be among them. An Ashkenazi Jewish delicacy, the baked good is famous for its eye-catching swirls of layered dough and ripples of sweet additions from cinnamon to chocolate. Traditional versions have a brioche-style crumb, while newer renditions lean croissant-like with laminated dough.

This babka is inspired by the celebrated Nutella babka from Breads Bakery. Only use finely chopped couverture or eating chocolate here, so it melts into the Nutella spread. One decadent bite and you can't stop.

⅓ cup (80 ml) lukewarm water
1 teaspoon dried yeast
1⅔ cups (250 g) all-purpose
 (plain) flour, plus extra for dusting
2 tablespoons superfine (caster) sugar
½ teaspoon fine sea salt
1 egg
1½ oz (40 g) unsalted butter, melted
½ cup (150 g) Nutella (or good-quality
 chocolate hazelnut spread)
2¾ oz (80 g) dark chocolate
 (55% cocoa solids), finely chopped

Sugar syrup
2 tablespoons superfine (caster) sugar

Place the water and yeast in the bowl of a stand mixer fitted with a dough hook and leave for 5 minutes, or until frothy. Add the flour, sugar, salt, egg, and butter and knead on low speed until the dough comes together. Increase the speed to medium and knead for a further 8 minutes, or until the dough is smooth and elastic. Transfer the dough to a greased bowl, then cover and set aside in a warm place for 1 hour, or until risen about one and a half times in size.

Grease a 10 in × 5 in (25 cm × 13 cm) bar (loaf) tin and line with baking paper.

On a lightly floured work surface, roll out the dough into a 14 in (35 cm) square. Spread the Nutella evenly over the dough, all the way to the edges, then scatter with the chocolate. Roll the dough tightly into a log, ending seam side down. Use your hands to evenly lengthen the log, so it's about 20 in (50 cm) long.

Using a serrated knife, cut the log in half lengthways. Twist the babka by crossing the two strands to form an X in the middle. Twist the strands at the top and bottom of the X, keeping the cut sides facing up, then fold the ends under to seal. Transfer to the bar tin, cover and stand in a warm place for 1 hour, or until risen.

Preheat the oven to 350°F (180°C).

To make the syrup, place the sugar and 2 tablespoons of water in a small saucepan over medium–high heat. Bring to the boil, stirring until the sugar dissolves, then remove from the heat.

Bake the babka for 20 minutes. Reduce the oven temperature to 300°F (150°C) and bake for a further 15–20 minutes, until the top is golden. Remove from the oven and brush generously with the syrup. Leave to cool in the tin and enjoy the same day.

Pancakes on Sundays

SERVES
2

A fixture on menus across the city, New York pancakes range from fluffy mile-high stacks to Dutch babies and thick old-school griddle cakes. While no one version reigns supreme, all conjure comfort, especially for brunch, when restaurants pull out all the stops. These Sunday-style flapjacks are light-as-air, drowned in syrup and finished with whipped salted honey butter—with a distinctive crisp edge from cooking in a generous pool of butter.

1 cup (150 g) all-purpose (plain) flour
1 tablespoon baking powder
2 tablespoons superfine (caster) sugar
½ teaspoon fine sea salt
2 eggs
1 cup (250 ml) buttermilk
2 teaspoons natural vanilla extract
4½ oz (125 g) unsalted butter, melted
warm maple syrup, to serve

Whipped honey butter

2½ oz (75 g) unsalted butter,
   chopped, softened
1 tablespoon honey
large pinch of sea salt flakes

Place the whipped honey butter ingredients in a large bowl. Using electric beaters, whisk until light and fluffy. Alternatively, whisk by hand.

Sift the flour, baking powder, sugar, and salt into a large bowl. Whisk the eggs, buttermilk, and vanilla extract in a separate bowl until smooth. Slowly whisk the wet ingredients into the dry ingredients until combined, then whisk in 2 tablespoons of the melted butter.

Heat an 8 in (20 cm) heavy-based frying pan over medium–low heat until hot (to ensure the pancake edges crisp up). Add 1 tablespoon of the melted butter, then add ½ cup (125 ml) of the batter. Cook for 2 minutes, or until the top of the pancake starts to bubble and the edges are slightly crisp. Carefully flip the pancake and cook for 1–2 minutes, until puffed and golden. Transfer to a plate and repeat with the remaining melted butter and batter.

Stack two warm pancakes on each plate and top with a spoonful of the honey butter. Pour over maple syrup to drown and serve immediately.

Cinnamon rolls

MAKES
12

New York mornings mean a hot cup of black coffee and breakfast pastries—and few are more classic or loved than the cinnamon roll. At coffee counters and bakeries, you'll find them generously swirled with brown sugar and spice, endlessly soft with just-baked brioche and decadently frosted with cream cheese or icing.

These rolls are baked in butter and drowned from top to side in a cream-based vanilla glaze, in true NYC style.

2 teaspoons dried yeast
1 cup (250 ml) lukewarm milk
½ cup (110 g) superfine (caster) sugar, plus an extra 1 teaspoon
3⅓ cups (500 g) all-purpose (plain) flour, plus extra for dusting
1 teaspoon fine sea salt
2¾ oz (80 g) unsalted butter, chopped, softened
2 eggs

Cinnamon filling

⅔ cup (150 g) brown sugar
1 tablespoon ground cinnamon
pinch of fine sea salt
2¾ oz (80 g) unsalted butter, softened

Vanilla glaze

1¼ cups (155 g) confectioners' (icing) sugar
⅓ cup (80 ml) pouring cream, at room temperature, plus a little extra if needed
1½ oz (40 g) butter, melted
2 teaspoons natural vanilla extract

Place the yeast, milk, and the 1 teaspoon of sugar in a bowl and set aside for 5 minutes, or until frothy.

Place the flour, salt, butter, eggs, and remaining ½ cup (110 g) of sugar in the bowl of a stand mixer fitted with a dough hook. Add the yeast mixture and knead until combined, then knead for another 5 minutes, until the dough is smooth and elastic. (It will be quite soft and sticking to the bottom of the bowl, but not the sides; add an extra 1–2 tablespoons flour if necessary.) Transfer the dough to a greased bowl, then cover and set aside in a warm place for 1 hour, or until doubled in size.

To make the cinnamon filling, combine the sugar, cinnamon, and salt in a bowl and set aside.

On a lightly floured work surface, roll out the dough into a 16 in × 12 in (40 cm × 30 cm) rectangle, about ¼ in (5 mm) thick. Gently spread the softened butter over the dough, then sprinkle the cinnamon mixture evenly over the top.

From the long edge closest to you, roll the dough into a tight log, finishing with the seam side down. Using a serrated knife, cut the log into 12 even pieces. Place the pieces, scroll-side up, in a baking tin lined with baking paper, then cover and stand in a warm place for 30 minutes, or until doubled in size.

Preheat the oven to 350°F (180°C). Bake the rolls for 25–28 minutes, until the tops are just golden. Cool the buns in the tin for 10 minutes, then turn out onto a wire rack to cool.

Combine the vanilla glaze ingredients in a large shallow bowl. The glaze should be a slightly runny consistency; if needed, add an extra 1 teaspoon of cream at a time to loosen it.

Dip each cinnamon scroll into the glaze to coat the top and sides, then place on the wire rack to set. Serve fresh.

Biscuit eggs benedict

SERVES
4

The birthplace of eggs benedict, New York has been turning out renditions of this classic since the 1880s, when it is said to have been created—either at the Waldorf Hotel or Delmonico's restaurant, depending on your source.

Today, few dishes epitomize the sacred weekend ritual of brunch more than two perfectly poached eggs sheathed in prime bacon and crowned with buttercup-yellow hollandaise sauce—here, soul food–style with a pinch of cayenne for heat, and on top of crumbly, buttery biscuits.

The secret is ensuring all the elements are perfectly warm, so prepare the biscuits, bacon, and hollandaise, and gently reheat if needed.

1 tablespoon olive oil
8 slices maple-cured Canadian
   or middle bacon
8 eggs
splash of vinegar
snipped chives, to garnish
pinch of cayenne pepper, to taste

Biscuits

1⅔ cups (250 g) all-purpose
   (plain) flour, plus extra for dusting
2 teaspoons baking powder
1 teaspoon superfine (caster) sugar
1 teaspoon salt
3½ oz (100 g) cold unsalted butter,
   chopped
1 cup (250 ml) pouring cream

Quick hollandaise

2 egg yolks
1 teaspoon lemon juice
1 teaspoon white wine vinegar
3½ oz (100 g) unsalted butter,
   melted and warm

Preheat the oven to 350°F (180°C). Line a baking tray with baking paper.

To make the biscuits, use a stand mixer with the paddle attached to beat the flour, baking powder, sugar, salt, and butter on low speed until the mixture is well coated and sand-like. Add the cream and beat until combined. Gently bring the dough together on a lightly floured work surface, then pat out until the dough is 1 in (2.5 cm) thick. Cut the dough into four 3½ in (9 cm) rounds using a floured cookie cutter, gently bringing the scraps together to create another biscuit, if necessary. Place on the baking tray and bake for 20–25 minutes, until puffed and golden.

Heat the olive oil in a large frying pan over medium heat. Fry the bacon, in batches, for 2 minutes on each side, until golden. Transfer to a plate and cover to keep warm.

Poach the eggs in a saucepan of simmering water with a splash of vinegar over medium heat until soft-poached (2½ minutes), then drain on paper towel.

Meanwhile, make the quick hollandaise. Use a stick blender to process the egg yolks, lemon juice and vinegar in a small saucepan (off the heat) until slightly thickened. With the motor running, gradually add the melted butter until emulsified—don't add it too quickly; the sauce should be slightly less thick than mayonnaise. Keep warm over very low heat until needed.

To assemble, split the biscuits in half and divide among four serving plates, split side up. Top each biscuit half with a slice of bacon and a poached egg. Drizzle with the hollandaise and season with salt and pepper. Garnish with chives and a pinch of cayenne pepper, and serve.

Morning

Brunch Bloody

MAKES
1

The bloody Mary, created sometime in the early 20th century, has origins as varied as iterations, from New York Bar in Paris to New York's St Regis Hotel. In any case, modern-day versions are a favorite companion to brunch in NYC, when cocktails are bottomless or at least savored for hours—the savory–spicy drink-slash-meal both hangover cure and restorative for the night ahead.

This recipe starts with a glass rim rubbed with Tajin, a Mexican blend of smoked chilies and lime, and finishes with green olives skewered with tangy pepperoncini.

1 cup (250 ml) good-quality
   tomato juice
2 dashes of Worcestershire sauce
2 dashes of Tabasco sauce
pinch of cayenne pepper
pinch of sea salt flakes
pinch of celery salt
pinch of freshly cracked black pepper
2 lemon wedges
¼ cup (60 ml) vodka or mezcal
ice cubes
1 tablespoon Tajin
2 pitted green olives
1 large pepperoncini (pickled golden
   Greek pepper)

Pour the tomato juice into a cocktail shaker. Add the Worcestershire and Tabasco sauces, cayenne pepper, salt flakes, celery salt, pepper, and the juice from one lemon wedge. Stir to combine, then taste and adjust the seasonings as needed. Add the vodka and fill with ice, then shake vigorously.

Place the Tajin on a small plate. Rub the rim of a 10 fl oz (300 ml) tumbler with the remaining lemon wedge, then turn in the Tajin to coat.

Fill the tumbler with ice, then strain the cocktail mixture over the top. Spear the olives and pepperoncini with a cocktail stick and place on top of the glass. Serve immediately.

Huevos rancheros verdes

SERVES
4

When the traditional Mexican breakfast, huevos rancheros (rancher's eggs), crossed the border into the United States, it became a staple in restaurants of every kind across the country. In New York, it's a brunch classic; the same hearty satisfying qualities meant for fueling farmers for the day, making it the perfect weekend reviver for city-bound New Yorkers.

Huevos rancheros look like a luscious pool of sauce, the stack of warm corn tortillas and yolky fried eggs hidden under roasted chili-licked salsa. This one is drowned in a salsa verde made with tart tomatillos, with a crumbly queso fresco topping and a pool of black beans on the side.

8 large corn tortillas
¼ cup (60 ml) vegetable oil
8 eggs
2 avocados, sliced
5½ oz (150 g) queso fresco or mild feta, crumbled
cilantro (coriander) leaves, to serve
lime wedges, to serve

Tomatillo salsa verde

1 lb 12 oz (800 g) tin tomatillos, drained
½ onion, finely chopped
3 garlic cloves, finely chopped
2 scallions (spring onions), thinly sliced
1 jalapeno, finely chopped, plus extra to serve
½ bunch cilantro (coriander), leaves chopped
2 teaspoons dried oregano
1 teaspoon cumin seeds

Frijoles negros

1 tablespoon vegetable oil
1 small onion, finely chopped
3 garlic cloves, finely chopped
2 × 14 oz (400 g) tins black beans, rinsed and drained
1 cup (250 ml) vegetable stock

Place all the tomatillo salsa verde ingredients in a saucepan with ¼ cup (60ml) of water. Bring to a simmer over high heat, breaking up the tomatillos with a wooden spoon, then reduce the heat to medium and cook for 15 minutes, or until the mixture is thickened. Remove from the heat and season with salt and pepper.

To make the frijoles negros, heat the vegetable oil in a saucepan over medium heat. Cook the onion, stirring, for 4 minutes, or until softened. Add the garlic and cook for 1 minute, or until fragrant. Add the beans and vegetable stock, then bring to a simmer and cook for 3 minutes or until warmed through, mashing some of the beans to thicken slightly; the mixture should be slightly soupy. Remove from the heat and season with salt and pepper. Keep warm.

Heat a large frying pan over medium–high heat until hot. Warm the tortillas in batches for 1 minute on each side, or until softened. Remove from the pan and wrap in a clean tea towel to keep warm.

Heat half the vegetable oil in the frying pan over high heat. Crack in four eggs and cook for 3 minutes for sunny side up, or until the whites are crisp around the edges and the yolks are still runny, spooning over a little hot oil as they cook. Repeat with the remaining oil and eggs.

Overlap two warm tortillas on each plate. Top with the eggs and drown in the salsa verde. Top with a few avocado slices and some extra jalapeno, then generously scatter the queso over. Pile the frijoles on the side of each plate and serve topped with cilantro leaves, and lime wedges on the side.

Challah French toast

SERVES
4

As Ashkenazi Jews made their way across Central and Eastern Europe, challah—a term for bread used as an offering—combined with local baking traditions to become the yellow-tinted, sweet, yeasted, six-strand braided beauty known and loved by American Jews. In New York, this style of challah is cherished by all and is a favored alternative to traditional bread—especially in the brunch icon, French toast.

These thick slices of challah are soaked in a creamy mix with cinnamon and orange zest, then deep-fried until crusted. Dust with icing sugar, drizzle with maple syrup, and serve with raspberry conserve for morning-meets-dessert heaven.

4 eggs, lightly beaten
1 cup (250 ml) pouring cream
1 cup (250 ml) milk
2 tablespoons superfine (caster) sugar
1 teaspoon ground cinnamon
zest of 1 orange
6–8 slices plain challah, each
  2 in (5 cm) thick
vegetable oil, for deep-frying
confectioners' (icing) sugar, for dusting
raspberry conserve and maple syrup,
  to serve

Crack the eggs into a large bowl and whisk lightly. Add the cream, milk, sugar, cinnamon, and orange zest, and whisk to combine. Working in two batches, add the challah slices and gently push down to submerge. Soak for 10 minutes turning them over halfway.

Heat a large saucepan one-third full with vegetable oil over high heat to 320°F (160°C).

Remove the challah slices from their soaking liquid, draining well. Deep-fry in batches, turning occasionally, for 1–2 minutes on each side, until golden and crisp. Drain on paper towel.

While still warm, dust the challah French toast with confectioners' sugar and dollop with raspberry conserve. Drizzle with maple syrup to serve.

Chocolate chip cookies for days

MAKES
10

New York is a city of cookie lovers. In almost every cafe, bakery, and even restaurant, you'll find a house cookie on offer, enjoyed from breakfast until late at night. The deservedly famous purveyors—Jacques Torres Chocolate, Levain Bakery and Maman—and their unique takes on the cookie have spread across the world, but the inventiveness doesn't end there.

If there was one flavor that elicits Gotham's devotion, it's chocolate chip. This cookie—generous in size, perfectly round, chewy yet soft, and studded throughout with chocolate—follows in these footsteps, with an addictive sprinkling of hazelnut meal and roasted hazelnut chunks.

7 oz (200 g) unsalted butter, melted
10½ oz (295 g) brown sugar
⅓ cup (75 g) superfine (caster) sugar
1 egg
2 teaspoons natural vanilla extract
1⅔ cups (250 g) all-purpose (plain) flour
1 cup (100 g) hazelnut meal
1 teaspoon baking soda
1 teaspoon baking powder
1 teaspoon fine sea salt
7 oz (200 g) dark chocolate, roughly chopped
⅓ cup (50 g) roasted skinless hazelnuts, roughly chopped

Using a stand mixer or electric beaters, beat the melted butter and sugars in a bowl until well combined. Add the egg and vanilla extract and beat until glossy.

Sift the flour, hazelnut meal, baking soda, baking powder, and salt into a separate bowl and mix well. Add the dry ingredients to the wet ingredients and beat on low speed until just combined. Add the chocolate and roasted hazelnuts and stir until just combined.

Line two baking trays with baking paper. Using a large ice-cream scoop or spoon, measure out the dough into 10 balls, weighing about 4½ oz (120 g) each. Place on the baking trays 2 in (5 cm) apart. Refrigerate for 20 minutes to firm up.

Meanwhile, preheat the oven to 350°F (180°C).

For perfect circle-shaped cookies, place each dough ball in a 4 in (10 cm) metal egg ring and press the dough right to the edge. Bake for 14 minutes, or until the tops are golden. Remove from the oven and gently work any cookie that's risen over the edge back into the ring, so it's easy to remove once cooled.

Alternatively, bake as balls for 14–16 minutes, until golden and crisp around the edges.

Cool on the baking trays for 10 minutes, then transfer to a wire rack to cool completely. Remove the rings from the cookies and serve.

167 W 74TH ST, NEW YORK,
NY 10023

Famous New York Cookies

Pam Weekes &
Connie McDonald

I was born in New Rochelle and grew up on Long Island, but I always knew I would end up in New York. My parents worked here and both of my grandfathers owned businesses in the city (Pam).

I was born in Upstate New York. I was always fascinated with the city, but never spent a huge amount of time here. I moved to New York City in 1983 and feel as though this is where I really grew up (Connie).

We started Levain Bakery in 1995. We both knew that we wanted to run our own businesses. When we were training for triathlons, particularly an Ironman race, we had lots of time to chat on our bikes and discuss ideas—none of which was a bakery! I have always loved baking and Connie discovered after going to culinary school and working in restaurants that she also loved it. So when we saw an opportunity, we jumped on it.

Our first retail location was on the Upper West Side of Manhattan. At the time we were really looking for an affordable space and West 74th Street was it. It was in a residential neighborhood with some great local food shops, including Fairway, Citarella, and Zabars. We loved the thought of being part of a community and people's lives. Over the past almost 30 years, we have made so many good friends, gotten to know lots of families and watched children grow up, some even working at the bakery.

We have so many memorable stories. Recently, one even gained national attention. We always put aside a whole-wheat raisin roll in a bag with the name of a customer who has been coming in almost daily for the roll and a chat. One day, the talented staff decided to start beautifully decorating the bag for him. *People Magazine* got wind of it and the 'Don Bag' was born!

Starting a business in New York is challenging, period. Yet it is also one of the best places in the world to do it because people here are so curious, enthusiastic, and interested in small neighborhood places. We now have 14 bakeries across the country, but we try to make sure that each location feels like the original shop—a part of the neighborhood and local community.

We both love to share and the size of our cookies is perfect for two. We started making them for ourselves prior to opening the bakery as a delicious treat after big workouts. Our best-selling cookie is always our chocolate chip walnut—the original!

We produce and bake them fresh all day long in our bakeries, so you are pretty much guaranteed a warm cookie. We have also donated all daily leftovers since day one. We like to think that we were an important part of the beginning of cookie culture in New York. Everyone loves cookies— they are classic.

Visitors always seem a bit surprised to learn that New Yorkers are so nice. We are not sure why—of course we are! If you haven't been, you should definitely visit. New York is the best place in the world.

COOKIES · CAKE · BROWNIES · PIES · COFFEE

Menu

 EST 1995

 EST 1995

Pastries & Brioche

Plain Brioche	$3.25
Blueberry Muffin	$4.50
Chocolate Chip Brioche	$5.00
Cinnamon Butter Brioche	$5.00
Oatmeal Raisin Scone	$4.00
Lemon Slice	$4.75
Banana Chocolate Chip Slice	$4.75
Sour Cream Coffee Cake Slice	$4.75

Cookies

Chocolate Chip Walnut	$5.25
Dark Chocolate Chip	$5.25
Oatmeal Raisin	$5.25
Dark Chocolate Peanut Butter Chip	$5.25
Two Chip Chocolate Chip	$5.25
Vegan & GF Chocolate Chip Walnut	$6.25
Caramel Coconut Chocolate Chip	$5.25
Lemon	$5.75

Loaf

Banana Chocolate Chip Loaf	$27.50
Sour Cream Coffee Cake Loaf	$27.50
Lemon Loaf	$25.00

Breads

Country Roll	$1.00
Baguette with Butter & Jam	$4.00
Country Baguette	$3.25
Country Boule	$6.00
Whole Grain Loaf	$7.00
Whole Wheat Walnut Raisin Loaf	$7.00

Beverages

Espresso Drinks	$5.25
Cold Brew	$5.25
Hot Tea/Iced Tea	$5.25
Valrhona Hot Chocolate	$5.25

Caramel Coconut Chocolate Chip Cookies

NOON

◆◆◆

As lunchtime hits, New York swells with life. Whether working from home in Brooklyn or in a Midtown office, locals love lunch and stepping back into the rhythm of the city. During the work week, favorites include a low-brow, high-flavor combo of street carts, take-out counters and food halls, where service is lightning fast and people of all ages and walks of life cross paths.

These venues offer more than just delicious food; for different migrant communities they're a comforting taste of home. From Jewish delis and Italian salumerias to curb-side halal carts and dosa trucks, these cherished spots form the backbone of the city, and many are now woven into the fabric of New York's food culture. Pastrami on rye, Italian hero, falafel pita—a few hallmark contributions to the city of sandwiches—all started here.

If there's a touch more time to spare, there's the lunch counter and luncheonette. More casual than a restaurant and more elevated than a diner, luncheonettes combine counter seating with concise menus and modern takes on nostalgic classics, with tomato soup and grilled cheese come fall, and refreshing salads in summer.

In 1979, an editor at *Esquire* coined the term "power lunch" to describe the vibrant midday dining scene at the Four Seasons hotel in New York. While the tradition of expense account–friendly restaurants continues to this day, it has also evolved, with bustling chef-driven cafes and charming venues from West Village to Ridgewood.

Outdoor dining has also changed the face of lunch. Once a temporary solution to rebuild hospitality in the city, sidewalk tables in brownstone-lined streets, secret garden courtyards, and backyard spaces in Brooklyn are now permanent fixtures—and make lunch paired with people watching a treasured new pastime.

Street cart soft pretzels

MAKES
6

In America, pretzels first made landfall in Pennsylvania with German immigrants who arrived at the turn of the 1700s. A century later, a second wave of migrants brought pretzels to New York, peddled in beer halls in Little Germany on the Lower East Side and then in street carts around the city. Today they are one of New York's most enduring street snacks, the large rings conveniently stacked on rods to grab, or warmed in a heated cabinet on vendors' carts. The best are soft yet slightly chewy, with a dark golden skin from being boiled before baking, slow-fermented for a richly flavored dough, and speckled with fat crystals of salt.

2 teaspoons dried yeast
1⅓ cups (330 ml) lukewarm water
2 tablespoons dark brown sugar
4 cups (600 g) bread flour, plus extra
    for dusting
1¾ oz (50 g) unsalted butter, melted
2 teaspoons fine sea salt
¼ cup (70 g) baking soda
1 egg, lightly beaten
pretzel salt or coarse sea salt flakes,
    for sprinkling

Place the yeast, water, and 1 teaspoon of the sugar in a bowl and set aside for 5 minutes, or until foamy.

Place the flour, butter, salt, and remaining sugar in the bowl of a stand mixer fitted with a dough hook. Mix on low speed until combined. Add the yeast mixture and knead until combined, then knead on medium–high speed for 6 minutes, or until smooth and elastic. Transfer the dough to a greased bowl and cover with plastic wrap.

For a cold-fermented version, refrigerate overnight, or for up to 1 day, to develop the flavor. Alternatively, leave the dough in a warm place for 1 hour, or until risen, but not doubled in size.

Line two baking trays with baking paper. On a lightly floured work surface, roll the dough out into an 18 in × 10 in (45 cm × 25 cm) rectangle. Using a sharp knife, cut the dough lengthways into six 1½ in (4 cm) wide strips. Roll one strip into a 20 in (50 cm) long, even rope that's slightly thinner at the ends. Fold the rope into a pretzel shape by forming a 'U', overlap the ends twice, then flip the ends down and seal behind the base of the U. Transfer to one of the prepared trays and repeat with the remaining dough. Cover the trays and set aside in a warm place for 45 minutes.

Preheat the oven to 430°F (220°C).

Fill a large saucepan one-third full of water. Add the baking soda and bring to a simmer over medium–high heat. In batches, carefully add the pretzels, top side down, to the water. Cook for 10 seconds, then gently flip over and cook for a further 10 seconds. Using a slotted metal spatula, transfer to the trays. Brush the pretzels with the egg and sprinkle with salt.

Transfer to the oven and bake the pretzels, swapping the trays halfway, for 15 minutes, or until deep golden. Serve warm.

Noon

Tuna melt

MAKES
2

The tuna melt sandwich wasn't created in New York, but is certainly among its comfort-food favorites. It joins a line of satisfying creamy salad fillings, from tuna salad with crunchy, peppery celery, to egg salad with fresh dill—and even the double, combining the two in distinct layers—served in bagel sandwiches and hero rolls.

The melt takes it up a notch with a blanket of sharp melted cheddar and a warm, rather than cool, finish between two buttered slices of whole-wheat bread or sourdough crisped until golden on a griddle. In true diner fashion, it's served with a handful of kettle-style chips, which you can enjoy on the side, or stuff into the sandwich for crunch.

butter, for spreading
4 slices whole-wheat (wholemeal) bread or sourdough
3½ oz (100 g) sharp cheddar, grated or sliced
dill pickles and kettle-style potato chips (crisps), to serve

Tuna salad
7 oz (200 g) tin good-quality tuna in oil, drained well
1 celery stalk, finely chopped
1 tablespoon finely chopped onion
⅓ cup (80 g) whole-egg mayonnaise
2 teaspoons freshly squeezed lemon juice
1 teaspoon honey
1 teaspoon dijon mustard

Combine all the tuna salad ingredients in a bowl. Season with salt and pepper and mix well.

Spread the butter over one side of all the bread slices. Turn the slices over, then divide the cheese between two bread slices and top with the tuna salad. Sandwich with the remaining two bread slices, buttered side up.

Heat a large frying pan over medium heat. Place the sandwiches in the pan and cook, pressing once with a spatula, for 3 minutes on each side, or until the bread is golden and toasted and the cheese has melted.

Cut the sandwiches in half on the diagonal and serve warm, with a dill pickle and a handful of potato chips.

Italian hero sandwich

MAKES
4

The first "heroes"—then known as an Italian sandwich and now simply referred to as sandwich—were made in the late 19th century for southern Italian laborers hungry for a taste of home. The fresh foot-long crusty rolls stuffed with Italian cured meats and sliced Italian cheese assuaged appetites, spreading from Hell's Kitchen to other Italian neighborhoods across the city.

Today, the inclusion of lettuce, pepperoncini, roasted bell pepper (capsicum), a splash of vinegar, and a drizzle of olive oil—and not much more—is said to define the true Italian hero of New York from other American body-length sandwiches, hoagies, subs, and grinders. The genre has expanded, of course, from riffs on cold heroes to hot heroes with chicken parms, meatballs, and more.

This hero combines a classic combo of cold cuts, sliced buffalo mozzarella, and peppery rocket with a punchy herb dressing—but you can swap in an aged balsamic for equal effect. As is custom, wrap your heroes in deli paper to hold it all together, and enjoy.

4 long white crusty "hero" rolls, about 8 in (20 cm) long, warmed

1 lb 2 oz (500 g) thinly sliced mixed Italian cold cuts, such as capicola, soppressata, mortadella, and ham

9 oz (250 g) buffalo mozzarella, drained, sliced

1 small red onion, thinly sliced

2 plum (roma) tomatoes, thinly sliced

5½ oz (150 g) pepperoncini (pickled golden Greek peppers), thickly sliced, plus a little brine for drizzling

4½ oz (125 g) baby arugula (rocket)

Herb dressing

1 bunch of parsley
8 garlic cloves
1½ tablespoons dried oregano
½ cup (125 ml) extra virgin olive oil
⅓ cup (80 ml) white wine vinegar
1 teaspoon white sugar

To make the herb dressing, use a stick blender to whiz all the ingredients, along with 1 tablespoon of water, until combined. (Or, simply finely chop the parsley and garlic, place in a bowl with the remaining ingredients and water, and stir to combine.) Season with salt and pepper.

Cut the warm rolls in half lengthways, leaving one edge attached so they're butterflied. Place on individual large sheets of baking paper or foil.

Spread some of the herb dressing on the bottom half of each roll. Layer the cold cuts over the inside of the butterflied rolls. Top with the mozzarella, onion, tomato, pepperoncini, and a drizzle of brine from the pepperoncini jar.

Toss the remaining herb dressing through the rocket, then divide among the rolls; it will feel like it's not going to fit, but everything will compress once sandwiched. Wrap each hero tightly in the baking paper or foil to secure.

Stand for 5 minutes for the flavors to combine, then cut in half crossways to serve.

27 ORCHARD ST, NEW YORK,
NY 10002

Lower East Side's
Family-Owned
Italian Deli

Roman Grandinetti

I was born and raised in Bensonhurst, Brooklyn, the same neighborhood that my father grew up in. We even went to the same schools. At home, my family cooked dinner every night and we always hosted family, and then friends as the years went by, for all the holidays. As a kid, I would help my mother in the kitchen—there was always something to do—and as I grew, I became more interested in cooking (although I'm sure I also did enough eating to learn).

I'd had the idea for Regina's Grocery for a long, long time. Delis and their culture are slowly dying in the city. Mom-and-pop shops are closing or getting pushed out because of rent. I own a creative agency and work with a ton of creatives, so I thought if we can develop brands successfully for other people, then maybe we are

good at what we do. I started making sandwiches and inviting friends over to try them.

I named the business after my mother because she's an amazing cook and friend. I picked Orchard Street for our first location because I thought it was going to be *the* next neighborhood. There aren't many parts left in NYC where that's still happening. Neighborhoods change, but Orchard Street really developed culturally just as we were moving in. And, of course, with that change comes your everyday characters, people who my mother feels she has to look out for. There's always something happening or someone yelling.

We opened Regina's to supply the area with a safe space for some good food and to join in the family. Covid

was a stand-out time for us—we remained open every day and donated more than 5,000 sandwiches. It really gave true meaning to the shop.

Now that we have four stores, our days are a bit crazy. It starts with a call to Mom about where she will be and any news on the day, then I speak to Jose Vasquez (who is like my brother) about what needs to get done and find out what store he will be in. Then we are off! You wait 'till about noon for the rush to start and then enjoy an espresso around 4 pm when it's all over.

A sandwich in New York is something everyone understands and there is always something for everyone. We don't love to customize a sandwich but ... no cheese, no problem; extra oil, sure thing; make it spicy, with pleasure.

We sell hundreds of sandwiches every day, but I think what really draws people is the experience of meeting my mom and taking a picture with her. My mother's Calabrian chili spread is famous and what made the shop—we add it to some sandwiches, but so many people ask for it as an extra. For me, the perfect hero sandwich is always simple, always quality and always from the heart! If not that, there's always the meatball special.

REGINA'S *Classic*

01
UNCLE JOHN

Prosciutto, Provolone, Mortadella,
Hot Sopressata, Lettuce, EVOO,
Red Wine Vinegar & Roasted Reds
on Classic Hero

$19⁰⁰

02
LIL PHIL

Smoked Ham, Provolone,
Lettuce, Tomato
on Classic Hero

$16⁵⁰

03
COUSIN ANTHONY

Smoked Chicken, Fresh Mozz, Arugula,
Balsamic, EVOO on Classic Hero

$18⁰⁰

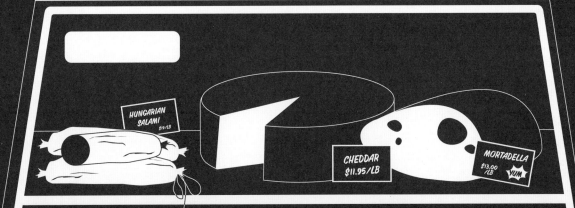

HUNGARIAN
SALAMI
$19/LB

CHEDDAR
$11.95/LB

MORTADELLA
$13.00
/LB

YUM

BACON
$11.95/LB

JARLSBERG
$17.95/LB

Seasonal Produce

Bodega chopped cheese

MAKES
4

For decades known only to New Yorkers, the chopped cheese sandwich—or "chopped cheese"—came out of Harlem in the 1990s and became a bodega favorite for lunch and drunken late-night meals in boroughs across the city. With beef patties, onions, and American cheese cooked on a hot grill until darkly browned, vigorously chopped to swirl the melted cheese through and toppled onto a long, chewy roll with lettuce and tomato, it combines the best traits of a burger, cheesesteak, and hero sandwich, all in one. Take a moment to admire the gooey cheesy layers before digging in.

1 lb 2 oz (500 g) ground (minced) beef
2 teaspoons smoked paprika
1 teaspoon garlic powder
1 teaspoon onion powder
1 teaspoon brown sugar
2 tablespoons olive oil
1 onion, thinly sliced
8 slices American cheese
4 hero or round crusty rolls, split
whole-egg mayonnaise and ketchup, for spreading
1 small iceberg lettuce, shredded
6 plum (roma) tomatoes, sliced

Pickled jalapenos

2 fresh jalapeno chilies, sliced into thin rounds
2 tablespoons apple cider or white vinegar
2 teaspoons white sugar
1 teaspoon sea salt

In a small bowl, mix together all the ingredients for the pickled jalapenos. Set aside for 10 minutes to pickle.

Place the beef, paprika, garlic powder, onion powder, and sugar in a bowl. Season well with salt and pepper. Use your hands to combine, then shape into four patties.

Heat 1 tablespoon of the olive oil in a large frying pan over high heat. Add two patties and scatter half the onion in the pan. Pressing the patties with a spatula to flatten them, cook for 2 minutes, or until well browned. Turn the patties over and toss the onion. Cook for 2 minutes, or until well browned. Using a spatula, chop up the patties, tossing in the onion. Top with half the cheese slices, cover with a lid and cook for 30 seconds, until the cheese has almost melted.

Meanwhile, toast two of the rolls in a sandwich press until almost crisp. Spread both cut sides generously with mayonnaise, then drizzle the bottom half with ketchup.

Divide the beef mixture among the rolls. Top with lettuce, tomato and pickled jalapenos and drizzle with a little of the pickling liquid. Roll tightly in baking paper or foil and stand for at least 2 minutes.

Repeat with the remaining ingredients to make four sandwiches. Cut in half to serve.

The Reuben

MAKES
4

The story of the Reuben starts with pastrami, which arrived with Romanian Jews in the mid-19th century. Today, the hopelessly rich and tender cut of smoked brisket is thick-sliced by hand, then piled decadently high between two slices of rye bread with a kick of mustard and nothing more—a throne for the moist meat, and decidedly New York's most iconic sandwich known simply as "pastrami on rye".

In 1914, Arnold Reuben broke kosher tradition by combining meat and cheese—and an American adaptation was born. The deli classic combines similarly fatty slices of warm corned beef with added tangy kraut, Russian dressing, and melted Swiss cheese for a sandwich and meal in one. Over the decades, other iterations have evolved, including the "Rachel" with turkey instead of corned beef.

Each component is straightforward, but you can substitute store-bought sliced corned beef and sauerkraut for a quicker take.

8 slices rye bread
butter, for spreading
8 slices Swiss cheese

Corned beef

1 lb 12 oz–2 lb 3 oz (800 g–1 kg) corned brisket (with fat cap, if available)
1 carrot, roughly chopped
1 onion, roughly chopped
1 celery stalk, roughly chopped
1 teaspoon black peppercorns
1 fresh bay leaf

Quick kraut

1 tablespoon olive oil
½ onion, thinly sliced
¼ white cabbage (about 10½ oz/300 g)
½ cup (125 ml) apple cider vinegar
1 teaspoon caraway seeds
1 teaspoon superfine (caster) sugar
½ teaspoon fine sea salt

Russian dressing

⅓ cup (80 g) whole-egg mayonnaise
2 tablespoons sour cream
1½ tablespoons prepared horseradish
1 tablespoon finely chopped onion
1 tablespoon finely chopped gherkin
1 teaspoon Tabasco sauce or ketchup

Place all the corned beef ingredients in a large saucepan. Cover with cold water, bring to the boil, then reduce the heat to low. Simmer for 2 hours, or until the beef is tender. Remove from the heat, then leave the beef to rest in the water for 30 minutes.

Meanwhile, to make the quick kraut, heat the olive oil in a saucepan over medium heat. Cook the onion for 3 minutes, or until softened. Stir in the remaining ingredients and 2 tablespoons of water. Reduce the heat to low and cook, covered, for 10 minutes, or until softened. Set aside to cool.

Preheat the oven to 400°F (200°C).

Combine the Russian dressing ingredients in a bowl and season with salt and pepper. Drain the brisket from the water and thickly slice across the grain.

Toast the bread lightly in a toaster. Spread one side of each slice with butter, then flip them over and spread with the Russian dressing. Top half the bread slices with a slice of cheese, corned beef, drained sauerkraut and another slice of cheese, then sandwich with the remaining bread, buttered side up.

Transfer to a lined baking tray and bake for 5 minutes, or until the cheese has melted. Cut in half and serve immediately.

QUALITY
SANDWICHES

FRESH
FRESH
FRESH

Classic

HERO
COMBOS

Now
OPEN

ORDER AT THE COUNTER!

MENU

Chicken parm $11.95

BREADED CHICKEN, MARINARA SAUCE, MOZZARELLA

Turkey provolone $15.95

ROASTED TURKEY, MAYO, ARUGULA, PROVOLONE

Meatball $17.95

MEATBALLS, MARINARA SAUCE, PARMESAN

Club $20.95

CHICKEN, BACON, LETTUCE, TOMATO, MAYO

Grilled cheese & tomato soup combo

SERVES
4

The grilled cheese sandwich—better known as "grilled cheese"—rose in popularity during the Great Depression and World War II, when pasteurized Kraft cheese and mass-produced sliced white sandwich bread, invented earlier in the 20th century, were combined for a simple yet satisfying meal. The New York comfort food is still made this way, slathered with mayonnaise for a golden crust, thick with gooey American cheese and served hot off the griddle with a dill pickle at diner counters. It's also elevated with a blend of aged and melting New York State cheeses, or sandwiched between crusty sourdough, the cheese seeping through the airy crumb.

It's also partnered with homestyle tomato soup for dunking or slurping on the side—a hallowed tradition for cold, rainy, or need-a-pick-me-up days, making it soothing comfort food like nothing else.

Make as separate snacks, or together for a generous meal.
It's good any which way!

8 slices sourdough, about ½ in (1.5 cm) thick
2¾ oz (80 g) salted butter, softened
dijon mustard, for spreading
7 oz (200 g) vintage cheddar, grated
5½ oz (150 g) firm mozzarella, grated

Tomato soup

4½ oz (125 g) salted butter, chopped
2 onions, roughly chopped
2 tablespoons all-purpose (plain) flour
4 × 14 oz (400 g) tins diced tomatoes
½ cup (125 ml) vegetable stock
1 tablespoon granulated sugar
⅓ cup (80 ml) pouring cream, plus extra to serve
chili flakes, to serve

To make the tomato soup, melt the butter in a large saucepan over medium–low heat. Add the onion and cook, stirring occasionally, for 15 minutes, or until very soft (do not brown). Add the flour and stir for 1–2 minutes, until golden. Add the tomatoes, stock, and sugar, and season generously with salt and pepper. Bring to a simmer, then reduce the heat to low. Cook, stirring occasionally, for 25 minutes, for the flavor to develop. Remove from the heat and stir in the cream. Using a stick blender, process until smooth. Just before serving, gently reheat, until warmed through.

To make the grilled cheese, heat a large frying pan over medium heat until hot. Spread one side of each bread slice with the butter. Turn four of the bread slices buttered side down, lightly spread with mustard and top with the cheeses. Sandwich the remaining slices on top, buttered side up. Working in batches, cook the sandwiches in the pan, pressing down lightly with a spatula so the bread browns evenly, for 3 minutes, or until golden and crisp underneath. Turn the sandwiches over and cook for another 3 minutes, or until the bread is golden and the cheese has melted. Remove from the pan and cut in half on an angle.

Divide the tomato soup among bowls and swirl with a little extra cream. Season with salt and pepper, scatter with chili flakes, and serve alongside the grilled cheese.

114

Waldorf salad with a view

The first waldorf salad was served on March 14, 1893, at the hotel Waldorf Astoria's debut event. The elegant combination of four ingredients—apple and celery tossed in good-quality mayonnaise over a bed of lettuce—was designed for New York's elite, but through the 20th century became an American staple known the world over. The dish is credited to maître d'hôtel Oscar Tschirky, who wasn't a chef, but was nevertheless a celebrity in his own right during his tenure at the Waldorf, and later published the recipe in a cookbook. Not long after, walnuts became an accepted topping; today, additions span from chicken and grapes to candied nuts.

While the chilled salad is no longer a common sight in New York, its culinary influence lives on.

2 granny smith apples

1 teaspoon freshly squeezed lemon juice

4 celery stalks, thinly sliced, inner heart leaves reserved

7 oz (200 g) red seedless grapes, halved

9 oz (250 g) baby romaine (cos) lettuce, leaves separated

1 cup (100 g) walnuts, toasted

¼ cup snipped chives or finely chopped parsley leaves

Lemon mayonnaise

2 egg yolks

½ teaspoon finely grated lemon zest

2 tablespoons freshly squeezed lemon juice

¾ cup (185 ml) mild-flavored olive oil or sunflower oil

2 teaspoons superfine (caster) sugar

½ teaspoon sea salt flakes

To make the lemon mayonnaise, process the egg yolks, lemon zest, and juice in the bowl of a food processor until combined. Gradually add the oil in a thin, steady stream until the mixture is thick and emulsified, adding 1–2 tablespoons of water as it thickens. Add the sugar and salt, season with pepper, and process until combined. Refrigerate until chilled.

Core the apples, but don't peel them. Using a sharp knife, cut them into julienne strips and toss them in a bowl with the lemon juice to stop them browning. Place the apple, celery (and leaves), grapes, and lettuce in separate bowls, and set aside in the fridge to chill.

When ready to serve, arrange the lettuce, apple, celery (and leaves), and grapes among plates. Drizzle with the lemon mayonnaise, then scatter with the walnuts and chives. Season with salt and pepper, and serve.

Manhattan clam chowder

SERVES
4

Inlets around New York have been clamming spots for centuries, which is where the city's love for the chewy briny mollusc can be traced back to. Two styles of clam chowder eventually took root: New England and Manhattan, the former white from a milk or cream base, and the latter red from tomatoes.

Believed to be the influence of Italian migrants on the city's cuisine, tomatoes and dried chili flakes bring beautiful acidity, sweetness, and heat to chowder, balancing the natural salinity of clams, while potatoes, which cook in the broth, help thicken the finished dish. Manhattan clam chowder is less common in the city today, but the flavors here make a wonderful case for revival.

Discard the clam shells before serving, if you prefer, and serve with traditional oyster crackers.

¼ cup (60 ml) olive oil
5½ oz (150 g) speck
   or bacon, chopped
1 onion, finely chopped
2 carrots, finely chopped
2 celery stalks, finely chopped
4 garlic cloves, thinly sliced
2 teaspoons thyme leaves
¼ teaspoon chili flakes
2 cups (500 ml) dry white wine
2 lb 3 oz (1 kg) clams, rinsed
2 × 14 oz (400 g) tins crushed tomatoes
14 oz (400 g) all-purpose potatoes,
   peeled, cut into 1¼ in (3 cm) chunks
1 fresh bay leaf
finely chopped parsley, to serve
traditional oyster crackers,
   to serve (optional)

Heat 1 tablespoon of the olive oil in a large saucepan over medium heat. Cook the speck or bacon, stirring, for 8 minutes, or until the meat is golden and the fat has rendered. Remove the speck, leaving the fat in the pan.

Add the remaining olive oil to the pan, along with the onion, carrot, and celery. Season with salt and pepper and cook, stirring, for 6–8 minutes, until soft. Add the garlic, thyme, and chili flakes and stir for another 1 minute, until fragrant.

Pour in the wine and 1 cup (250 ml) of water and bring to a simmer over medium–high heat. Add the clams, cover and cook for 5 minutes, or until the shells have opened. Using a slotted spoon, remove the clams and set aside in a bowl, discarding any unopened shells.

Add the tomatoes, potato, and bay leaf to the broth, season with salt and pepper and bring to the boil. Reduce the heat to medium and cook, partially covered, for 15 minutes, or until the potato is tender.

Using a fork, gently mash one-third of the potato to thicken the broth. Stir in the clams and bacon and cook for another 3 minutes, or until warmed through. Season with salt and pepper. Divide the clam chowder among bowls, scatter with parsley, and serve with oyster crackers scattered over the top, if desired.

Matzo ball soup

SERVES
4

Quintessential comfort food, matzo ball soup is a Jewish deli favorite and a common addition to a Passover Seder. The appeal lies in the glistening soup, rich and aromatic yet light on the tongue, a spattering of just-tender thinly sliced vegetables, and the simple soothing dumplings (known as "knaidlach" in Yiddish), which give way like a cloud with each spoonful. There are various views on permitted additions—from poached chicken (which is also used to make the broth) to short noodles—as well as the actual texture of the matzo balls themselves, from denser "sinkers" to lighter "floaters". This rendition falls into the former camp, served as a single centerpiece ball in each bowl of vegetable-based soup.

1 tablespoon vegetable oil
1 carrot, halved lengthways, thinly sliced
1 celery stalk, thinly sliced
3 garlic cloves, thinly sliced
8 cups (2 litres) vegetable stock
olive oil, for drizzling
dill fronds, to serve

Matzo balls

4 eggs
¼ cup (60 ml) vegetable oil
¼ cup (60 ml) vegetable stock or water
1 cup (120 g) matzo meal
¼ teaspoon ground nutmeg
½ teaspoon ground cinnamon
1 teaspoon ground ginger
1 tablespoon finely chopped parsley
1 teaspoon fine sea salt

Place all the matzo ball ingredients in a bowl. Season with black pepper and stir to combine. Cover and refrigerate for at least 3 hours.

Bring a large saucepan of salted water to the boil. Using wet hands, shape the matzo mixture into four equal-sized balls. Add the matzo balls to the water, return to a simmer and cook for 20–25 minutes, until al dente. Remove using a slotted spoon, discarding the water.

Meanwhile, to make the soup, heat the vegetable oil in a separate saucepan over medium heat. Cook the carrot and celery for 5 minutes, or until soft. Add the garlic and cook for 1 minute, or until fragrant. Pour in the stock and bring to the boil, then reduce the heat to medium–low and cook for 10 minutes to develop the flavor. Remove from the heat and season with salt and pepper.

Divide the soup and matzo balls among four bowls. Drizzle with a little olive oil, then scatter with dill and season with black pepper to serve.

Falafel house sandwich

MAKES
4–6

A wave of Arab immigrants arrived in the United States in the late 1960s, including Syrian-born Mamoun and Maria Chater, who opened the first falafel restaurant in New York and helped pioneer Middle Eastern food throughout the country. Mamoun's is still an institution, and the countless falafel houses and carts in the city reflect the rich spread of migrant groups across the boroughs, from Lebanese and Turkish to Egyptian and Israeli. The falafel sandwich is the signature order, joining Gotham's canon of hand sandwiches, with a trademark touch from each vendor.

The house twist here is green tahini, with lengths of fresh scallion and a kick of harissa or hot sauce to finish. Prepare the green tahini ahead, so you can enjoy the falafels piping hot and crunchy, straight from the pan.

Before making the falafels, you'll need to soak the dried garbanzo beans overnight.

canola oil, for deep-frying
4–6 pita pockets, warmed until soft
2 short cucumbers, diced
2 truss tomatoes, diced
2 scallions (spring onions), halved
   lengthways, then cut into
   2½ in (6 cm) lengths
hot sauce, or harissa loosened
   with vegetable oil, to serve

Falafels

9 oz (250 g) dried garbanzo
   beans (chickpeas)
½ cup cilantro (coriander) leaves
½ cup parsley leaves
1 small onion, roughly chopped
4 garlic cloves, peeled
1 long red chili, seeds removed,
   roughly chopped
2 tablespoons sesame seeds
1 tablespoon all-purpose (plain) flour
1½ teaspoons sea salt
1 teaspoon baking powder
1 teaspoon ground cumin

Green tahini

½ cup (135 g) tahini
juice of 1 lemon
1 garlic clove, chopped
½ cup parsley and cilantro (coriander)

To make the falafels, soak the garbanzo beans in a large bowl of cold water for at least 12 hours, changing the water once or twice.

Drain the garbanzo beans well, then place in a food processor with the herbs, onion, garlic, and chili. Season with black pepper, then process until very finely ground, but not a paste; you may need to scrape down the side of the bowl and add 1–2 tablespoons of water for a smooth consistency. Add the remaining ingredients and process until just combined.

Using a stick blender or food processor, blend the green tahini ingredients and ¼ cup (60 ml) of water together until smooth. Season with salt and set aside.

Fill a large saucepan one-third full with canola oil and heat over medium heat to 350°F (180°C).

Scoop heaped tablespoons of the falafel mixture and shape into 20 balls or patties. Working in batches, cook the falafels in the oil for 4 minutes, or until golden and crisp. Drain on paper towel.

To assemble the sandwiches, cut the pita pockets in half crossways, open them up and spread some green tahini inside each one. Crush a falafel in each pita, then loosely fill with more falafels (about two in each half, depending on the size of your pita breads). Pile in the cucumber and tomato and top with the scallion, then generously spoon more green tahini over the top. Drizzle with hot sauce or harissa to serve.

Iceberg wedge salad

SERVES
4

The wedge salad—dressed quarter-moons of crisp iceberg lettuce—is indispensable steakhouse fare. Since at least the middle of the last century, its attractive form and fresh tart flavors have been the perfect companion to a rich prime rib off the grill, or a main in its own right for a power lunch at a light-filled village restaurant.

This wedge is classic in form, with both a vinaigrette and blue cheese dressing, finished with crisp bacon pieces and juicy cherry tomatoes.

7 oz (200 g) thick-cut bacon slices, cut into ½ in (1 cm) chunks
1 large head of iceberg lettuce, outer leaves removed
7 oz (200 g) cherry tomatoes, halved
½ bunch of dill, fronds picked
crumbled blue cheese, to serve

White wine vinaigrette

½ cup (125 ml) extra virgin olive oil
¼ cup (60 ml) white wine vinegar
2 French shallots, thinly sliced
2 teaspoons honey
1 teaspoon sea salt flakes

Blue cheese dressing

1¾ oz (50 g) blue cheese
½ cup (125 g) plain yoghurt
¼ cup (60 g) whole-egg mayonnaise
1 tablespoon freshly squeezed lemon juice

Place the bacon in a cold large frying pan over medium–high heat and cook until golden and crisp. Drain on paper towel.

Combine all the vinaigrette ingredients in a bowl. Season with pepper and set aside for 10 minutes to marinate the shallot.

In a separate bowl, mix together the blue cheese dressing ingredients until smooth. Season with salt and pepper, and chill until needed.

To assemble the salad, cut the lettuce into four wedges, removing the core. Divide the lettuce wedges and tomato among four plates. Drizzle with the vinaigrette and spoon the blue cheese dressing over the top. Scatter each wedge with the bacon, dill and crumbled blue cheese, and serve immediately.

Noon

POTATO LATKES WITH
- **SALMON ROE & CREME FRAICHE** 16
- **APPLESAUCE & SOUR CREAM** 10

CHEESE BLINTZES WITH BLUEBERRY COMPOTE 15

MATZO BALL SOUP 8

MUSHROOM BARLEY SOUP 7

CHILLED BORSCHT 7

Latke platter

MAKES 6 LARGE
OR 12 SMALL LATKES

Among the city's iconic Jewish dishes are latkes. The potato pancakes are traditionally served at Hanukkah, but you can also find them throughout the year for the many devotees at restaurants. Latkes' magic lies in their deeply golden crisp exterior and soft shoestring-like center—achieved by squeezing the grated potato and onion well to remove the excess moisture, and adding just a touch of matzo meal or flour to bind.

Serve as crunchy squares or rustic rounds, as they are here, with traditional creme fraiche and applesauce for dipping into, and smoked salmon and horseradish to slather on top for a mix-and-match platter.

1 lb 2 oz (500 g) floury potatoes, such as sebago or russet, peeled
½ large onion
canola oil, for shallow-frying
1 egg
2 tablespoons matzo meal or all-purpose (plain) flour
1 teaspoon sea salt flakes, plus extra to serve
½ teaspoon freshly cracked black pepper

To serve

applesauce
creme fraiche or sour cream
horseradish cream or freshly grated horseradish
smoked salmon
snipped chives
lemon wedges

Coarsely grate the potatoes and onion. Wrap them in a clean tea towel, and wring tightly to squeeze out as much liquid as possible.

Fill a large deep frying pan ½ in (1 cm) full of canola oil and heat over medium–high heat until hot and shimmering.

In a large bowl, lightly beat the egg. Add the potato mixture, flour, salt, and pepper and stir until well combined. For large latkes, divide the mixture into six even portions, then shape each one into a rectangle about ½ in (1 cm) thick, pressing to compact. Alternatively, use a ¼ cup (60 ml) measure to make 12 small round latkes.

Working in batches, carefully transfer the latkes to the hot oil using a spatula. Cook for 4 minutes, or until golden on the bottom, then flip over and cook for a further 4 minutes, or until golden and crisp. Drain on a plate lined with paper towel and sprinkle with more salt.

Serve the latkes warm, with pots of applesauce, creme fraiche, and horseradish, and smoked salmon, chives, and lemon wedges on the table for everyone to serve themselves.

Smash burgers

MAKES
4

By some accounts, hamburgers have been a part of the city from as early as 1820, when patties were sold by waterfront vendors to homesick German sailors. So, it's no surprise New York is home to some of the world's best burgers, and that they come in various guises, from thick and fancy to quick and deliciously dirty. Of course, there's also Shake Shack, which started as a hot dog cart in Madison Square Park and turned its smash-style burgers into a global phenomenon.

These smash burgers use a heavy-based pan to develop their quintessential crust, some soft potato buns to give way to the patty, and homemade creamy tangy burger sauce to bring it together.

1 lb 2 oz (500 g) good-quality ground (minced) beef, with 20% fat
vegetable oil, for greasing
4 slices yellow American cheese
4 soft white potato rolls
butter, for spreading
4 oak or green leaf lettuce leaves
2 plum (roma) tomatoes, sliced

Burger sauce

⅓ cup (80 g) whole-egg mayonnaise
2 tablespoons ketchup
2 tablespoons American yellow mustard
2 tablespoons finely chopped sweet-sour pickles or cornichons
½ teaspoon garlic powder
½ teaspoon sweet paprika
¼ teaspoon cayenne pepper or chili powder

Combine the burger sauce ingredients in a bowl and set aside.

To make the patties, gently shape the beef into four even rounds, about 2 in (5 cm) wide and 2 in (5 cm) tall. Avoid overworking the meat, so your patties stay tender and juicy.

Lightly grease a large cast-iron or heavy-based frying pan with vegetable oil. Heat the pan over high heat until smoking. Generously season the patties all over with sea salt and black pepper. Add two patties to the pan and press firmly with a metal spatula, until about 4 in (10 cm) wide and ½ in (1 cm) thick. Cook for 60–90 seconds, or until a dark brown crust forms on the bottom.

Flip the patties over, ensuring you scrape up and capture all the crusty bits. Place a cheese slice on top of each and cook for 30 seconds, or until the cheese has melted and the meat is medium-rare. Remove from the pan and repeat with the remaining patties and cheese.

Split the potato rolls open and lightly toast them (you want them warmed, but not crisp). Lay them on your work surface, cut side up. Spread butter over each one. Layer the bases with the burger sauce, lettuce, tomato and the meat-cheese patties. Sandwich with the tops and serve immediately.

123 Madison St, New York,
NY 10002

Serving
Classic NY Diner
Dishes

Sam Yoo

I was born and raised in Queens. My parents ran a Korean barbecue restaurant, and it was a huge part of my life. I remember the energy of stepping inside a bustling restaurant— the clanging of plates, pots, and pans; roaring laughter wafting its way throughout the room, and a well-orchestrated staff handling the chaos with calm and dexterity.

I didn't know it back then, but once I hit the "age I needed to figure out my career," I quickly recognized that this addictive "bustling restaurant" energy was exactly what I wanted to surround myself with for years to come.

Working in New York, I met my mentors Rich Torrisi and Mario Carbone. I was fortunate to have met them early on when I was green as grass and they had one restaurant. I was able to grow with them, starting out as a young line cook learning their standards, picking up on their exacting eye for detail, and eventually opening restaurants side-by-side with them. Needless to say, these profound experiences formed my growth as a chef.

I always knew I wanted to be a creator and say my piece in this world. Weeks leading up to signing the lease for Golden Diner, I had a few opportunities to take on some very cushy private chef gigs. During this time I lost sleep thinking to myself, 'Do I really want to enter this arena, be subject to criticism by the masses, and potentially fail and be in debt for God knows how long?' It didn't take long for me to process these doubts as "normal" and conclude that the answer was a no-brainer.

Growing up in Queens, there were a plethora of diners. It's where you would go to hang out as a kid in junior high and high school, being too young to go to a bar. The concept of a diner being a place for people of all ages was very special for me—a third place for

137

the community. Diners were also a dying breed around the time I opened GD. They were closing left and right, so I wanted to use my fine-dining training as a chef to create a truly unique menu, filled with badass food, for ALL of the people.

For two years I went up and down the streets of Chinatown, knocking on every business owner's and landlord's door I could find, looking for a space. The place I eventually found had been a Puerto Rican social club in the 70s, which I found really cool, and a Chinese print shop in the last decade.

By our second year of opening, I was humbled and honored to receive local and national accolades. We were busy and it was difficult for me to stay present during all the madness as a first-time business owner.

But there was this one morning, just a chill weekday. I looked out into the dining room from our open kitchen and saw something that made me pause and take a breath of gratitude. There was an older Chinese couple eating breakfast with their family; hipsters who had recently moved into the area ordering from their server; and two police officers sitting by the counter sipping on their coffees. 'Yes! This is it!' I thought. Guests from all ages, ethnicities, and socioeconomic statuses were in this room, eating together. This was exactly what I envisioned and there it was right in front of me. I'll never forget that day.

Menu

Homemade Granola & Yogurt $11.00

Chinatown Egg & Cheese Sando $13.00

Two Eggs, How You Want 'Em $13.00

Golden Omelette $15.00

Breakfast Burrito $14.00

Honey Butter Pancakes $15.00

**Make it Deluxe! Serve with
French Fries & Pickles**

SIDES & ADD ONS

Yogurt		French Fries	
Avocado	$6.00	Home Fries	$9.00
Tofu Scramble	$4.50	Crispy Chicken	$10.00
2 Eggs	$5.00	Applewood Smoked Bacon	
Toast	$5.00	Pat LaFrieda Sausage	
Green Salad	$5.00	Red Cabbage Slaw	
Vegan NY Kimchi	$9.00	Pico de Gallo	
	$5.00		

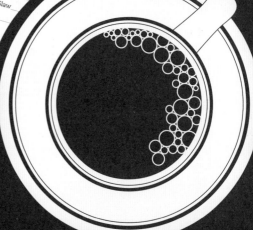

Golden Diner

New York's finest hot dog

MAKES
6

Hot dogs got their start in the 1860s, when German migrant Charles Feltman started slinging them in a pushcart on Coney Island, giving rise to an Americana favorite. In 1939, President Franklin Roosevelt even served Nathan's Famous, one of the city's best-known dogs, to visiting royal King George VI. A classic New York dog—affectionately known as 'dirty water dogs' for the salt and fat-licked cart water they're warmed in—is a relatively simple affair compared to other American city standards: an all-beef frankfurter in a soft warm bun with a handful of tangy kraut and spicy brown mustard. The defining addition, for many, are sauteed onions, deliciously heightened with sweet ketchup and spices.

6 beef hot dogs
6 hot dog buns, split, but not all
 the way through
1 cup (150 g) drained sauerkraut,
 warmed or at room temperature
spicy brown mustard or American
 yellow mustard, to serve
ketchup, to serve (optional)

Sweet spiced onions

2 tablespoons olive oil
2 large onions, sliced
2 tablespoons dark brown sugar
½ teaspoon ground cinnamon
½ teaspoon chili powder
pinch of cayenne pepper (optional)
¼ cup (60 ml) ketchup

To prepare the sweet spiced onions, heat the olive oil in a saucepan over medium heat. Add the onion and cook, stirring, for 5 minutes, or until soft. Add the remaining ingredients and ½ cup (125 ml) of water and stir to combine. Bring to a simmer, then cook for 10 minutes, or until the liquid has thickened. Remove from the heat and season with salt and pepper.

Meanwhile, bring a large saucepan of water to the boil. Add the hot dogs, reduce the heat to medium and cook for 5 minutes, or until warmed through. Remove from the water and drain in a colander.

Place the buns on their side, so the split is facing up. Slip the hot dogs in, then spoon the sauteed onion and sauerkraut over the top. Drizzle with your choice of mustard and/or ketchup to serve.

Halal cart lamb over rice

SERVES
4

From brightly colored trucks roaming the streets or from permanent curbside spots comes the alluring smell of spiced meat, charred on a hot griddle plate or carved from a searing rotisserie. Known generally as "halal food", "lamb over rice", "shawarma" or affectionately as "street meat", the dish comprises any combination of lamb or chicken (or both), with turmeric-hued rice, shredded lettuce and pops of chopped tomato with a heavy hand of "white" and "red" sauces—tahini-yoghurt and hot sauce and spices.

The dish in its current form evolved out of the 1980s and 90s with the arrival of Egyptian, Greek, and South Asian migrants, taking over hot dog carts and servicing Muslim taxi drivers in Midtown, blending flavors and ingredients from Pakistan to Trinidad with delicious effect—and creating a halal cart cuisine of its own.

1 lb 5 oz (600 g) boneless lamb leg, thinly sliced
1 teaspoon ground cumin
1 teaspoon ground coriander
1 teaspoon ground allspice
1 teaspoon ground cinnamon
2 tablespoons vegetable oil
1 small onion, finely chopped
2 garlic cloves, finely chopped
2 teaspoons finely grated ginger
shredded iceberg lettuce and sliced tomatoes, to serve

Yellow rice

1 tablespoon vegetable oil
½ onion, finely chopped
¾ in (2 cm) piece of ginger, finely grated
1 teaspoon ground turmeric
¼ teaspoon ground cardamom
2 cups (400 g) white basmati rice

White sauce

7 oz (200 g) plain yoghurt
1 tablespoon tahini
1 garlic clove, crushed
1 tablespoon lemon juice

Red sauce

1 tablespoon hot sauce
1 tablespoon ketchup

To make the yellow rice, heat the vegetable oil in a saucepan over medium heat. Cook the onion and ginger, stirring, for 5 minutes, or until soft. Season with salt and pepper. Add the turmeric and cardamom and cook for 1 minute, or until fragrant. Add the rice and stir until well combined. Pour in 2¾ cups (685 ml) of water, increase the heat to high and cover with a lid. Bring to the boil, then reduce the heat to low and cook for 12 minutes, or until the rice is tender. Remove from the heat and stand for 5 minutes. Taste and season with salt and pepper.

Place the white sauce ingredients and ⅓ cup (80 ml) of water in a bowl. Season with salt and pepper and stir to combine. In a small bowl, mix together the red sauce ingredients and 1 tablespoon of water. Set aside.

Combine the lamb, spices and 1 tablespoon of the vegetable oil in a large bowl. Heat the remaining vegetable oil in a large frying pan over medium heat. Cook the onion, stirring, for 5 minutes, or until soft. Add the garlic and ginger and cook for 1 minute, or until fragrant. Increase the heat to high, add the lamb and stir-fry for 10 minutes, or until well browned. Season with salt and pepper and remove from the heat.

Divide the rice, lamb, lettuce and tomato among bowls. Drizzle generously with the white sauce and red sauce to serve.

Noon

146 **Noon**

Daily special cherry pie

SERVES
8

You can trace the seasons in New York with pies, the fillings changing as the weather cools and warms, and local produce makes its way into farmers' markets: tart apple pies in autumn; rich pumpkin and pecan pies for the holidays; and vibrant berry and stone fruit pies in summer.

Cherry season is short but spectacular, starting with sour cherries and ending with luscious syrupy fruit—and these beautiful moments in time are captured in flaky buttery crusts and "daily special" pies at dedicated pie shops, lunch counters and restaurants.

If cherries aren't in season, par-cooking frozen cherries sets the juices so the filling is full of bright cherry liquor, but isn't too wet.

2 lb 3 oz (1 kg) fresh or frozen cherries, pitted
¼ cup (55 g) superfine (caster) sugar
¼ cup (55 g) brown sugar
¼ cup (30 g) arrowroot
2 tablespoons freshly squeezed lemon juice
1 teaspoon natural vanilla extract
vanilla ice cream, to serve

Pie dough

½ cup (125 ml) milk
1 tablespoon apple cider vinegar
13 oz (375 g) all-purpose (plain) flour, plus extra for dusting
1 tablespoon cornstarch (cornflour)
2 tablespoons superfine (caster) sugar
1 teaspoon fine sea salt
9 oz (250 g) cold unsalted butter, chopped
1 egg, lightly beaten
demerara sugar, for sprinkling

To make the pie dough, combine the milk and vinegar in a jug. Place the flour, cornstarch, sugar, and salt in a food processor and blend to combine. Add the butter and process until starting to combine. With the motor running, add the milk mixture and process until the dough just comes together, with chunks of fat still visible. Divide into two even discs, wrap in plastic wrap and refrigerate for at least 1 hour.

If using fresh cherries, place them in a bowl with the remaining filling ingredients (no par-cooking required).

If using frozen cherries, thaw them, then place them in a saucepan over medium–low heat and cook for 2–3 minutes, until the cherries lose some juice. Add the sugars and arrowroot and cook, stirring gently, for 1–2 minutes, until starting to thicken. Remove from the heat, stir in the lemon juice and vanilla extract, and set aside to cool.

Preheat the oven to 430°F (220°C). Grease an 8¾ in (22 cm) pie dish.

Roll out one disc of dough on a lightly floured work surface to a 12 in (30 cm) round, then use it to line the pie dish. Trim the overhanging pastry to ½ in (1 cm), then freeze the pie shell until needed.

Continued

Noon

Roll out the remaining dough on a lightly floured surface to a 10 in (25 cm) round. Transfer the cherry filling to the pie shell, then cover with the pie top. Trim the excess pastry, then fold the top under the pastry edge. Flute the edge with your fingers, or crimp with a fork.

Brush the pastry with the egg, then sprinkle demerara sugar over the top. Using a sharp knife, cut 4–6 slits in the top as steam vents.

Place the pie dish on a baking tray (to protect your oven from any juicy spills) and bake for 20 minutes. Reduce the oven temperature to 350°F (180°C) and bake for a further 30–40 minutes, until the pastry is golden and cooked through.

Remove from the oven and cool on a wire rack for at least 1 hour for the juices in the filling to set. Serve warm or at room temperature, with vanilla ice cream.

Noon

Black & white cookie

MAKES
12

Among the truly iconic Big Apple items is the black and white cookie. Its origins can be traced back to Bavarian migrant bakers in the early 1900s, and today is synonymous with the city's Jewish bakeries, which turn out the storied rounds for bodegas and bagel shops that sell them across town. Cookie in name, their texture is really closer to vanilla cake (said to be born of leftover cake batter at the bakery each day), and flavored with a dash of lemon zest and a warming note of almond extract. The black and white top is somewhere between set chocolate and soft glaze, depending on the venue, adding texture to each comforting bite. Whether that's a little black and white in each bite or not is up to you.

1¾ cups (260 g) all-purpose (plain) flour
2 teaspoons baking powder
½ teaspoon fine sea salt
4½ oz (125 g) unsalted butter, chopped, softened
1 cup (230 g) superfine (caster) sugar
2 eggs
⅔ cup (160 g) Greek-style or plain yoghurt
zest of 1 lemon
¼ teaspoon natural almond extract

White glaze

3½ oz (100 g) white chocolate, finely chopped
1 teaspoon vegetable oil

Black glaze

3½ oz (100 g) dark chocolate (55% cocoa solids), finely chopped
1 teaspoon vegetable oil

Preheat the oven to 350°F (180°C). Line two baking trays with baking paper.

Sift the flour, baking powder, and salt into a bowl and set aside. Using a stand mixer or electric beaters, beat the butter and sugar in a bowl for 5 minutes, or until light and fluffy. Add the eggs, one at a time, beating until well combined after each addition. Add the yoghurt, lemon zest, and almond extract and beat until combined. Add the flour mixture and beat until just combined; the batter will be thick.

Using an ice-cream scoop with a lever, dollop the batter onto the baking trays, 2 in (5 cm) apart, to make 12 cookies. Alternatively, use a ¼ cup (60 ml) measure, but the cookies won't be as round.

Transfer one tray to the oven and bake the cookies for 12 minutes or until just firm to the touch in the center. The tops will be pale, but the cookies will be slightly golden underneath. Repeat with the remaining tray of cookies.

Remove from the oven and cool on the trays for 5 minutes, then transfer to a wire rack to cool completely.

Meanwhile, place the glaze ingredients in separate small saucepans over low heat and stir until melted and combined. Transfer to separate small bowls and stand for 10 minutes, or until thickened slightly; the glazes should be a thick pouring consistency.

Turn the cookies over so the raised edge is on the bottom. Spoon the white glaze over one half of a cookie, scraping the edge to tidy it. Transfer to a tray lined with baking paper and repeat with the remaining cookies. Spread the black glaze over the other half of the cookies. Allow to set before serving.

Brooklyn blackout cake

SERVES
12–16

This cake is everything the name conjures—decadently rich, dark, and delicious, with layers of moist coffee-kissed chocolate cake, creamy chocolate pudding, and glossy glaze, making it one of the best chocolate cakes of all time, and inspiring chocolate desserts around the world. Invented by the Brooklyn bakery chain Ebinger's, the cake takes its name from the blackout drills of World War II, when city lights were dimmed and windows covered with black to prevent sightings by enemy planes.

◆◆◆

3 cups (450 g) all-purpose (plain) flour
3½ oz (100 g) unsweetened (Dutch) cocoa powder
1 tablespoon baking soda
1½ teaspoons baking powder
1 teaspoon fine sea salt
3 eggs
3 cups (660 g) superfine (caster) sugar
¾ cup (185 ml) vegetable oil
1½ cups (375 ml) buttermilk
1½ cups (375 ml) brewed coffee, at room temperature
2 teaspoons natural vanilla extract

Chocolate pudding

2 tablespoons superfine (caster) sugar
1½ cups (375 ml) milk
2 tablespoons cornstarch (cornflour)
pinch of fine sea salt
2 egg yolks
5½ oz (150 g) dark chocolate (55% cocoa solids), chopped
1 teaspoon natural vanilla extract
¾ oz (20 g) unsalted butter

Coffee chocolate glaze

9 oz (250 g) dark chocolate (55% cocoa solids), chopped
1¾ oz (50 g) unsalted butter, chopped
¼ cup (60 ml) strong brewed coffee
1 tablespoon glucose or corn syrup
1 teaspoon natural vanilla extract

To make the chocolate pudding, place the sugar and 1 cup (250 ml) of the milk in a saucepan over medium heat and bring almost to the boil. Place the remaining ½ cup (125 ml) of milk in a bowl, add the cornstarch, salt, and egg yolks and whisk until smooth. Gradually whisk in the warm milk mixture, then return the mixture to the pan. Cook, whisking constantly, until thickened. Remove from the heat. Add the chocolate, vanilla extract, and butter, whisking until melted and combined. Cover the surface with plastic wrap and refrigerate for 1 hour, or until cold.

Preheat the oven to 350°F (180°C). Grease two 8 in (20 cm) round cake tins and line the bases with baking paper.

Sift the flour, cocoa, baking soda, baking powder, and salt into a bowl and set aside. Using a stand mixer, beat the eggs and sugar until light and creamy. Add the oil and beat until well combined. Alternately add the flour mixture and the buttermilk until just combined, beating after each addition. Add the coffee and vanilla extract and beat until just combined.

Divide the batter between the cake tins. Bake for 60–70 minutes, until a skewer inserted into the center comes out clean. Remove from the oven and leave to cool in the tins for 10 minutes, then transfer the cakes to wire racks to cool completely.

For the coffee chocolate glaze, place the chocolate and butter in a saucepan over low heat and stir until melted. Remove from the heat and stir in the coffee, glucose, and vanilla extract until smooth and combined. Set aside until cooled to a pouring consistency.

Using a long serrated knife, trim the tops of the cakes to make them level. Cut each cake in half horizontally through the middle. Spread one cake layer with one-third of the chocolate pudding, then top with another layer of cake. Add another one-third of the chocolate pudding, then repeat this process and finish with the final cake layer, bottom-side up, to create a smooth top. Cover the top and side of the cake with the glaze. Chill for 1 hour to soak in the syrup and firm up, then cut into slices to serve.

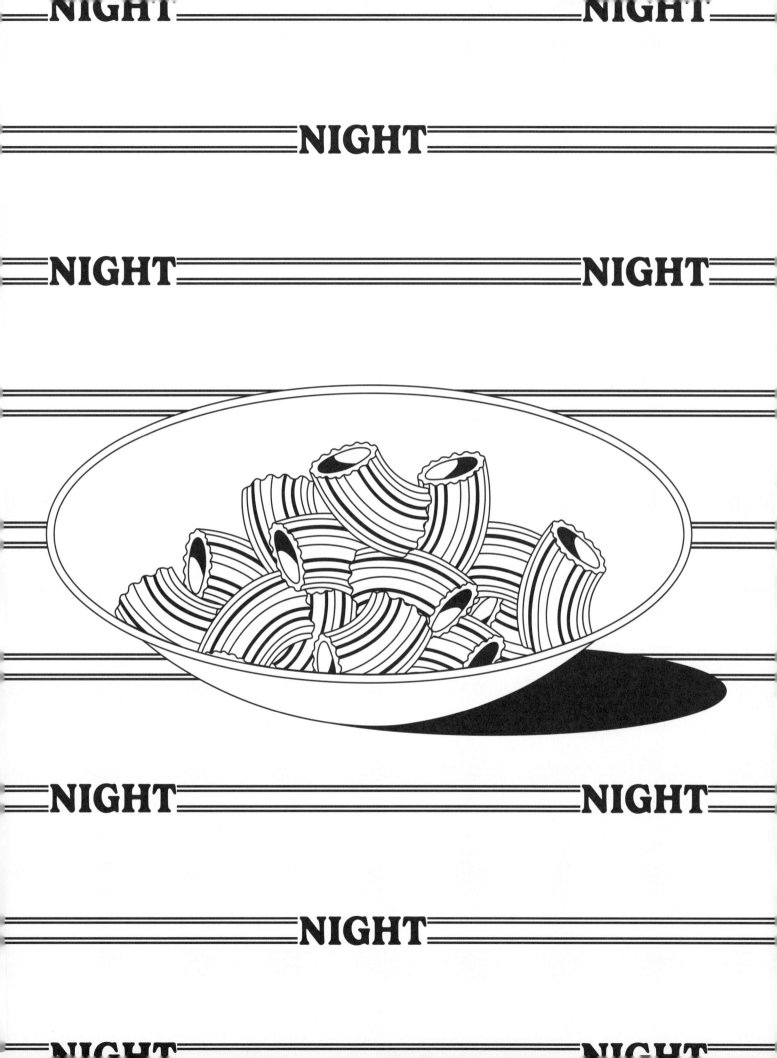

NIGHT

•••

As day turns to dusk and bright lights illuminate the streets and avenues, New Yorkers head out to eat and take on the night. Come twilight, outdoor dining spaces on sidewalks come to life and streets bustle every night of the week. A late-hours town by American standards, dinner doesn't usually hit its pace until 8 pm, and reservations can be made until 11 pm.

On any New Yorker's list of top dining spots will be a mix of decades-old establishments, different cuisines throughout the boroughs, late-night eats and exciting new hotspots. Their disparate qualities are the heart of Gotham's one-of-a-kind eating culture—one that's easily among the best in the world. One night it's a classic steakhouse or fine-dining favorite, another it's a ramen joint or communal Ethiopian restaurant. And each week, there's a new opening to feed the city's appetite.

Delmonico's, the first fine-dining restaurant in the country—credited for creating some of the city's now iconic dishes and drinks, including eggs benedict, baked Alaska, and the Manhattan cocktail—still thrives here, almost 200 years after first opening its doors.

The city's dives, rooftop bars, cocktail dens, and speakeasies offer the same escape and community for apartment-bound locals—a place to meet friends or take up a conversation with a stranger over a frosty beer or inventive concoction.

And if hunger follows—which it invariably does—late-night eats are on hand. From hole-in-the-wall "dollar slice" pizza and Indian chaat to full-blown feasts of dim sum in Chinatown, comfort food at a classic diner or elevated meals at celebrated restaurants, you can eat deep into the night and the early hours of the morning.

In the city that never sleeps, or at least only briefly, it's an experience that is truly in a world of its own.

Manhattan cocktail

MAKES
1

Invented in the late 1800s and imbibed by socialites of the time, the Manhattan quickly went on to become the most famous drink in the world. Considered the first modern cocktail for its combination of American whiskey, Italian vermouth, and a few dashes of aromatic bitters, its balanced and complex taste is still timeless today. Like anything with just a handful of ingredients, quality counts, as does technique—stirred, not shaken, perfectly chilled, and served in a coupe with a premium preserved cherry.

ice cubes
¼ cup (60 ml) rye whiskey
1 fl oz (30 ml) sweet vermouth
2 dashes of Angostura bitters
1 maraschino cherry

Fill a mixing glass with ice. Add the whiskey, vermouth and bitters and stir well to chill. Strain into a chilled coupe glass.

Garnish with the cherry and serve.

MANHATTAN

Cocktail

REVERSE MANHATTAN

2 PARTS VERMOUTH · 1 PART RYE WHISKEY
ANGOSTURA BITTERS

Green POINT

RYE WHISKEY
SWEET VERMOUTH
YELLOW CHARTREUSE
ANGOSTURA BITTERS
ORANGE BITTERS

BROOKLYN

RYE WHISKEY
DRY VERMOUTH

MARASCHINO
LIQUEUR

AMER PICON
(BITTER ORANGE APERITIF)

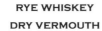
BLACK

Manhattan

RYE WHISKEY
AMARO
ANGOSTURA BITTERS
ORANGE BITTERS

RED HOOK

RYE WHISKEY
PUNT E MES (VERMOUTH)
MARASCHINO LIQUEUR

Enjoy

Happy hour oysters

SERVES
4

The port of New York was once home to thriving reefs and 200,000 acres of oyster beds. For about a century, oysters were among the city's most iconic dishes—ubiquitous, affordable, and sold across town in various guises, from high-end oyster cellars to street carts. Over-harvesting, foreshore development, and pollution contributed to the oysters' eventual demise, but the city's love for the bivalves lives on. Especially come summer, when iced trays filled with freshly shucked oysters glimmer on weekend brunch tables or happy hour bar counters, paired with classic accoutrements such as lemon, and inventive mignonettes like this one, studded with pretty pink peppercorns.

◆◆◆

24 oysters, shucked
lemon wedges, to serve

Pink peppercorn mignonette
2 teaspoons pink peppercorns
2 French shallots, finely diced
½ cup (125 ml) white wine vinegar
white pepper, for seasoning

To make the pink peppercorn mignonette, toast the pink peppercorns in a small dry frying pan over medium heat for 2 minutes, or until fragrant. Cool, then lightly crush using the side of a chef's knife or a mortar and pestle.

Combine the shallot and vinegar in a small non-reactive bowl and season with freshly ground white pepper. Cover and refrigerate overnight for the flavors to infuse.

Arrange the shucked oysters on an ice tray and serve with the mignonette and lemon wedges.

Night

Harlem fried chicken

SERVES
4–6

Blisteringly hot and shatteringly crisp, fried chicken is down-home comfort in every juicy bite. In New York, soul food's cultural home of Harlem is where eateries have been serving fried chicken over the counter since the neighborhood became a center for tens of thousands of Black Americans fleeing the south and Jim Crow laws in the early 20th century. Harlem is also where the enigmatic combination of fried chicken and waffles—often tied together with a dousing of maple syrup—is said to have originated. In any case, it was being served there by the mid-1930s, and today the pairing can be found throughout the city on brunch and diner menus.

Harlem-style fried chicken, textural from the cornmeal batter and tender from the buttermilk marinade, is also loved with a choice of soul food sides, from mac 'n' cheese to collard greens, and always with sauce: buffalo, barbecue, or hot spiced honey, as with this fried bird.

1 lb 5 oz–1 lb 12 oz (600–800 g) small boneless chicken thigh pieces, skin on, larger pieces cut in half
1½ cups (375 ml) buttermilk
2 teaspoons fine sea salt
canola oil, for shallow-frying
¼ cup (90 g) honey, or to taste
1 tablespoon hot sauce, or to taste

Cornmeal coating

1 cup (150 g) all-purpose (plain) flour
¼ cup (30 g) cornstarch (cornflour)
¼ cup (35 g) cornmeal (fine polenta)
1 tablespoon fine sea salt
2 teaspoons garlic powder
2 teaspoons onion powder
1 teaspoon sweet paprika
1 teaspoon freshly cracked black pepper

Place the chicken, buttermilk, and salt in a large bowl and stir to coat. Cover and marinate in the fridge for at least 1 hour, or up to 1 day.

Fill a large deep frying pan with about 2 in (5 cm) of canola oil. Heat over medium–high heat to 350°F (180°C).

Meanwhile, combine the cornmeal coating ingredients in a large shallow bowl.

Working with one piece at a time, remove the chicken from the buttermilk, allowing the excess to drip off. Turn to coat in the cornmeal mixture, patting it all over to ensure the chicken is well coated on all surfaces. Transfer to a plate and repeat with the remaining chicken.

Working in three batches, add the chicken to the hot oil and cook for 3 minutes on each side, or until deep golden and cooked through. Transfer to a plate lined with paper towel and rest for 5 minutes. Repeat with the remaining chicken, adjusting the heat to ensure that the oil returns to the right temperature before adding each new batch.

Combine the honey and hot sauce in a small saucepan over medium heat. Bring to a simmer, stirring to combine, then remove from the heat.

Serve the fried chicken with the hot spiced honey to glaze, drizzle or dip.

Night

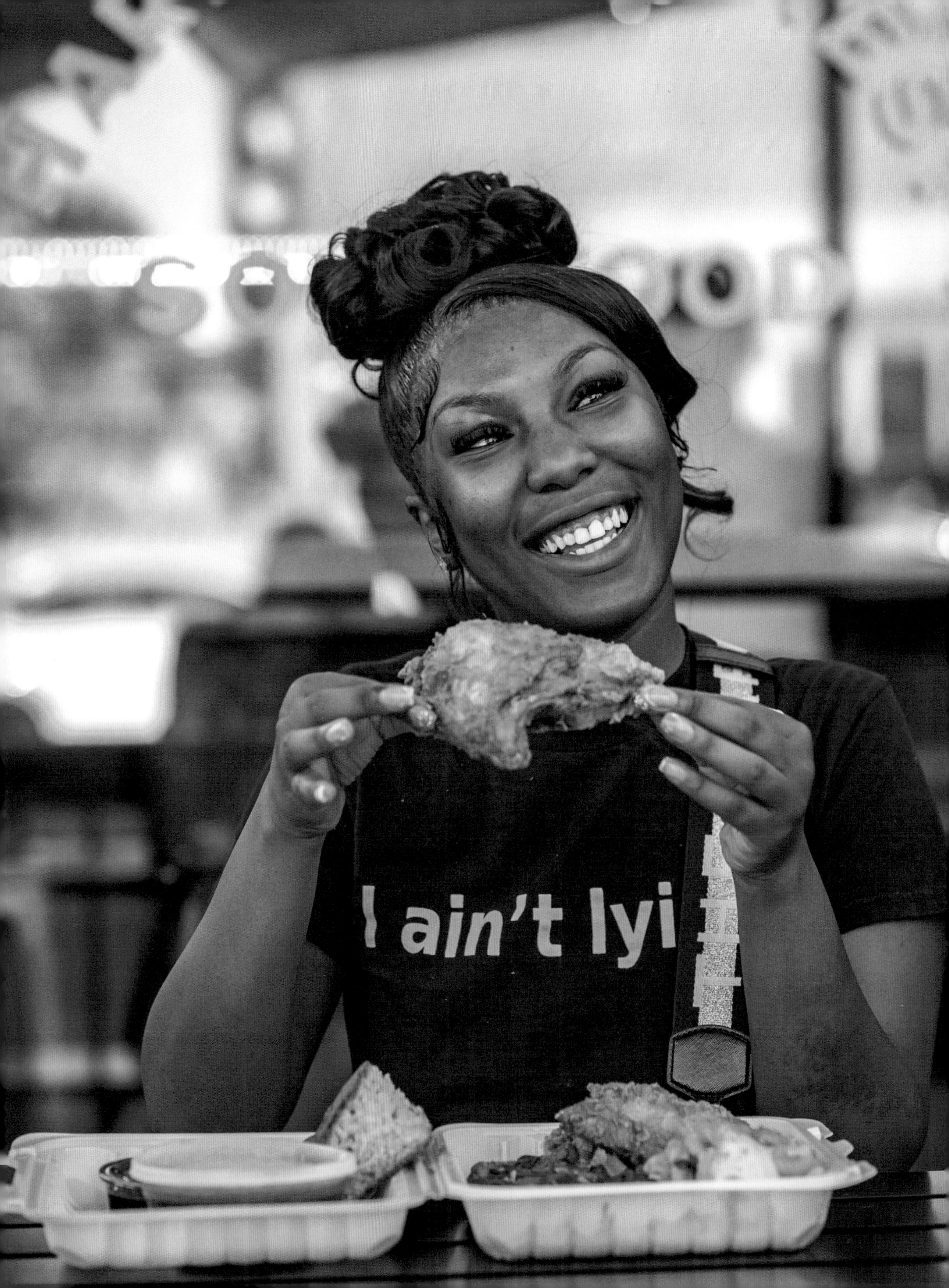
I ain't lyi

Chicken & avocado arepas

MAKES
4

Arepas, the traditional cornmeal cake of Venezuela and Colombia, arrived in New York City with migrants from both countries, finding homes in local communities in Astoria and Jackson Heights in Queens. The savory baked or fried rounds are comfort food from breakfast to night, eaten plain or as a side, or split and stuffed with a cacophony of fillings—from juicy shredded beef to fried plantains and black beans. In a city of sandwiches, arepas were a natural addition to the canon of cheap and satisfying hand-held options.

This timeless combination of shredded chicken, mayo, and avocado, known as "reina pepiada", is pretty much creamy chicken salad swirled with guacamole. For a vegetarian version, simply omit the shredded chicken and top the guacamole with grated queso blanco.

Arepas

2 cups (500 ml) warm water
2 teaspoons sea salt
2 cups (310 g) masarepa (pre-cooked white cornmeal, such as PAN Precocida)
1 tablespoon vegetable oil

Chicken avocado salad

1 large avocado
juice of 1 lime, plus extra wedges to serve
¼ cup (60 g) whole-egg mayonnaise
9 oz (250 g) poached chicken, finely shredded
½ small onion, finely chopped
¼ cup roughly chopped cilantro (coriander), plus extra to serve
½ fresh jalapeno chili, finely chopped, deseeded if desired, plus extra to serve

To make the arepas, place the water and salt in the large bowl of a stand mixer. With the mixer on low speed, gradually add the masarepa, then beat for 2–3 minutes; the dough will be soft, but not sticky, and will hold its shape without cracks at the side when formed into a disc. If it's too dry, add an extra tablespoon of water at a time. If it's too soft, add an extra tablespoon of masarepa at a time. Cover the bowl and stand for 15 minutes to hydrate.

Preheat the oven to 350°F (180°C). Divide the dough into four even portions, then shape each into a 4¾ in (12 cm) disc, about ½ in (1.5 cm) thick.

Warm half the vegetable oil in a large frying pan over medium–high heat. Add half the discs and cook for 5 minutes on each side, or until golden in parts and crisp on the outside. Transfer to the oven, placing them directly on an oven rack, and bake for 10 minutes, or until the arepas sound slightly hollow when tapped. (The inside may still be a little tacky in parts; this is fine.) Cook the remaining arepas in the same way.

Meanwhile, to make the salad, scoop the avocado flesh into a large bowl and roughly mash. Add the lime juice and mayonnaise, season well with salt and pepper and mash to combine. Stir in the remaining salad ingredients and set aside.

While the arepas are still warm, use a serrated knife to cut a slit around the edge to form a pocket, then stuff with the salad. Scatter with extra cilantro and chili, and serve with lime wedges.

Grandma slice

MAKES
16 SLICES

New York is well known for its round thin-crust pizzas, but there's another slice equally rooted in local pizza consciousness: grandma pie. Originating on Long Island and found only in metropolitan New York, it's named for the home-style pizzas originally made by Italian-American nonnas. Like Sicilian pizza or focaccia, the thick, fermented dough is stretched in a square pan, but left to rise for a shorter time—resulting in a slightly leaner, denser crust. The defining grandma trait is the olive oil–crisped base, which almost shatters against the light chewy top, as well as the diagonal spread of sauce, which ensures patches of tomatoey flavor, without weighing down the base.

3 garlic cloves, crushed
¾ cup (185 ml) olive oil
14 oz (400 g) fresh mozzarella, grated or sliced
14 oz (400 g) tin crushed tomatoes
2 teaspoons dried oregano
½ cup (50 g) finely grated parmesan
basil leaves, to serve

Pizza dough

3⅓ cups (500 g) bread flour
1 teaspoon dried yeast
2 teaspoons fine sea salt
1 tablespoon olive oil

To make the dough, place the flour and 13½ fl oz (400 ml) of room temperature water in a bowl and stir to combine. Stand for 15 minutes to rest. Add the yeast and stir to combine, then add the salt and oil and stir until well combined. Transfer to an oiled bowl, then cover and leave to stand for 10 minutes.

Reach underneath the dough and grab one-quarter of it. Gently stretch this portion of dough and fold it over the top, to the other side. Repeat with the remaining three corners of the dough, then turn the dough over and place seam side down. Stand for 10 minutes, then repeat this process twice. (Alternatively, after the first 15 minutes of standing, knead in a stand mixer with the dough hook attached for 7 minutes.)

Return the dough to the oiled bowl. Cover and refrigerate for at least 8 hours, but ideally 24 hours, to cold ferment.

Remove the dough from the fridge 1½ hours before using.

In a small bowl, combine the garlic and ¼ cup (60 ml) of the olive oil and set aside to infuse.

Coat an 18 in × 14 in (45 cm × 35 cm) rimmed baking tray with the remaining ½ cup (125 ml) of oil. (It may sound like an excessive amount of oil, but to get the authentic oil-crisped base, you need to glisten the pan well.) Instead of the baking tray, you could also use two 14 in × 9 in (35 cm × 23 cm) rectangular baking tins.

Continued
→

Night

Gently stretch the dough to cover the bottom of the tray, pressing the dough into the edges (you may need to set the dough aside to relax for a while, then try again). Cover the tray and stand for 30–40 minutes, or until the dough has puffed.

Meanwhile, place an oven rack in the lower third of the oven. Preheat the oven to 535ºF (280ºC), or as high as your oven will go.

Scatter the mozzarella over the dough, leaving a ¼ in (5 mm) border. Season the crushed tomatoes generously with salt and pepper, then dot them in diagonal lines on top, about 1½ in (4 cm) wide and 1¼ in (3 cm) apart. Bake for 18 minutes.

Remove from the oven, scatter with the oregano and parmesan, and drizzle with the garlic oil. Bake for a further 3 minutes, or until the base is golden and crisp.

Leave to rest for 5 minutes, then cut into 16 squares. Serve, scattered with the basil leaves.

Spicy mushroom ramen

SERVES
2

New York's first ramen house was Sapporo, but it's said the current phenomenon for ramen was ignited in 2004 with David Chang's Momofuku Noodle Bar, which leaned into the creative and artisan ramen boom in Japan at the time. Ramen shops are now found citywide, offering lean through to rich broths, thin and thick noodles and countless iterations—all quick to slurp down in summer, and the perfect foil for the cold come winter. Tonkotsu is perhaps the most common style, requiring days of patience for the broth to develop.

Blended until creamy, this vegetarian broth, inspired by a Lower East Side ramen house, is umami-rich from a mix of wild mushrooms. Add any vegetable toppings you please.

1 tablespoon vegetable oil
3 scallions (spring onions), thinly sliced, white and green parts separated
3 garlic cloves, chopped
1¼ in (3 cm) piece of ginger, finely grated
7 oz (200 g) mixed shiitake, enoki, oyster, and trumpet mushrooms, cut into thirds
2 cups (500 ml) vegetable stock
⅓ oz (10 g) dried kombu seaweed (about 2 pieces)
2 tablespoons white shiro miso paste
1½ tablespoons mirin
1 teaspoon sesame oil
1 teaspoon white sugar
ground white pepper, for seasoning
1 sweetcorn cob, in the husk
10½ oz (300 g) ramen noodles, cooked according to the packet directions
2 ramen eggs or soft-boiled eggs, halved
nori sheets and hot chili oil, to serve

Heat the vegetable oil in a saucepan over medium heat. Fry the white part of the scallion, stirring, for 2 minutes, or until softened. Add the garlic and ginger and cook for 1 minute, or until fragrant. Increase the heat to medium–high, add the mushrooms and stir-fry for 2 minutes, or until slightly browned.

Pour in the stock and 2 cups (500 ml) of water. Add the kombu and bring to a simmer, then reduce the heat to medium. Cover and cook for 15 minutes, or until the mushrooms are tender. Remove and discard the kombu.

In a small bowl, mix together the miso, mirin, sesame oil, and sugar until smooth, then add to the broth. Stir for about 1 minute, until melted and combined, then remove from the heat. Season with salt and white pepper.

Reserve one-quarter of the mushrooms for serving. Using a stick blender, blend the broth until creamy.

Meanwhile, microwave the sweetcorn cob in its husk for 2 minutes, or until tender. Remove the husk, then use a sharp knife to cut the kernels from the cob.

Divide the noodles among two bowls, then ladle the broth over. Arrange the corn, egg, green scallion, reserved mushrooms, and nori on top. Drizzle with chili oil to serve.

General Tso's chicken

Battered fried chicken pieces bathed in a moreish sauce, General Tso's chicken is a far cry from the original fiery Hunanese dish created by chef Peng Chang-kuei in 1955 for a US admiral's visit to Taipei, and named for the 19th century Chinese military hero General Tso Tsung-t'ang. As regional Chinese cuisine took hold in New York, chefs who'd tasted the original began serving it, albeit adapted to Americans' sweet, mild tastes. Peng eventually moved to New York in 1973 to find his dish significantly reimagined, but continued with the modified take in a restaurant of his own, helping popularize the dish both in New York and across the country, to become the takeaway option of choice in America today. The best renditions are crisp and tender, the satisfying sauce laced with a little heat, like this one here.

1 lb 2 oz (500 g) boneless, skinless chicken thighs or breasts, cut into ¾–1¼ in (2–3 cm) pieces
¾ cup (90 g) cornstarch (cornflour)
¼ cup (35 g) all-purpose (plain) flour
canola oil, for deep-frying
steamed white rice, to serve

General Tso's sauce

2 tablespoons shaoxing rice wine
2 tablespoons rice wine vinegar or white vinegar
⅓ cup (80 ml) soy sauce
1 teaspoon toasted sesame oil
¼ cup (55 g) superfine (caster) sugar
½ cup (125 ml) chicken stock or water
2 teaspoons cornstarch (cornflour)
1 tablespoon canola oil
8 small Chinese dried red chilies
3 garlic cloves, finely chopped
1 tablespoon finely grated ginger
2 scallions (spring onions), white parts thinly sliced, green parts thinly sliced on the diagonal

Marinade

1 egg white
1 tablespoon soy sauce
1 tablespoon shaoxing rice wine
1 tablespoon cornstarch (cornflour)

To make General Tso's sauce, place the shaoxing rice wine, vinegar, soy sauce, sesame oil, and sugar in a bowl. Combine the stock and cornstarch in a separate bowl, then stir into the soy sauce mixture. Set aside.

Place the marinade ingredients in a large bowl and whisk to combine. Add the chicken pieces, season with salt and pepper, and stir to coat.

Place the cornstarch and flour in a separate large bowl. Season with salt and pepper, and whisk to combine.

Fill a wok or large deep frying pan one-third full with canola oil and heat over high heat to 350°F (180°C).

Add one-third of the chicken (including the marinade, as the liquid will make crispy bits in the batter) to the cornstarch mixture and toss to coat, getting into all the nooks and crannies. Deep-fry the chicken for 3–4 minutes, until golden and crispy, turning halfway. Drain on a plate lined with paper towel and keep warm in a low oven. Working in two more batches, repeat with the remaining chicken.

To finish making the sauce, heat the canola oil in a large deep frying pan over medium heat. Stir-fry the chilies, garlic, ginger, and white part of the scallion for 3 minutes, or until soft and fragrant. Add the reserved sauce mixture and stir to combine. Bring to a simmer over medium–high heat until thickened, then add the fried chicken and toss to coat in the sauce.

Transfer the chicken to a serving bowl and scatter with the green scallion. Serve immediately, with steamed rice.

Aromatherapy
Photo-Light Therapy
Endermologie
Mineral Make-Up
Waxing Peels
Acne Specialists
Xi'an Famous Foods
WESTERN CHINESE CUISINE
NOW HIRING
OUR STORE ASSOCIATES
are paid $21.00-$24.50/hr
A
INSIDER

Spicy cumin lamb noodles

SERVES
2–3

Within the many Chinese enclaves in the city is the food of Shaanxi, a province at the eastern end of the ancient Silk Road, known for its fiery, spice-laden cuisine. Xi'An Famous Foods began selling specialties from the region at a stall in a Flushing mall and quickly expanded across New York as locals fell for the hand-pulled biang biang noodles rippled with chili oil and moreish, heavy-handed spicy cumin lamb. While both dishes are commonly found in parts of China, the crowd-pleasing two-in-one combo was born in New York at XFF.

For ease, this adapted recipe uses wide store-bought noodles with ground, toasted spices for intense flavor. Glossy and slippery with chili oil, this dish is a knockout.

9 oz (250 g) boneless lamb shoulder or leg
1 teaspoon cornstarch (cornflour)
¼ cup (60 ml) vegetable oil
1 tablespoon cumin seeds
2–3 Chinese small dried chilies
12½ oz (350 g) fresh pulled wheat noodles
4 garlic cloves, crushed
1 tablespoon finely grated ginger
3 scallions (spring onions), white parts thinly sliced, green parts cut into 1¼ in (3 cm) lengths
1 small onion, thinly sliced

Stir-fry sauce

¼ cup (60 ml) soy sauce
1½ tablespoons Chinkiang (Chinese black vinegar) or rice vinegar
1 tablespoon white sugar

Partially freeze the lamb (to make slicing much easier), then thinly slice with a sharp knife. Toss in a large bowl with the cornstarch and 2 teaspoons of the vegetable oil. Set aside.

Toss the cumin seeds and chilies in a small dry frying pan over medium heat. Toast for 2 minutes, or until fragrant. Grind to a powder using a spice grinder or mortar and pestle, then set aside.

Combine the stir-fry sauce ingredients in a bowl and set aside.

Bring a large saucepan of water to the boil. Cook the noodles according to the packet instructions. Drain, then rinse under hot water.

Heat 1 tablespoon of the remaining vegetable oil in a wok or large deep frying pan over medium–high heat. Stir-fry the garlic, ginger, and white part of the scallion for 30 seconds, or until fragrant. Add the lamb and stir-fry for 4 minutes, or until browned.

Stir in your ground cumin and chili and cook for 30 seconds, or until fragrant. Add the onion, green scallion and remaining vegetable oil, and cook for 1 minute, or until starting to soften. Finally, add the noodles and stir-fry sauce and toss to combine.

Remove from the heat, season with salt and pepper and serve immediately.

Above Spicy cumin lamb noodles

188

NOODLES & DUMPLINGS

饺子

麵條

BIG WONG
RESTAURANT

OPEN
MON, TUES, WED, THUR
8:30 am – 9:00 pm
FRIDAY – SUNDAY
8:30 am – 9:30 pm

OPEN 7 DAYS

NO.1
Xiao Long Bao

NO.1 .... **$9.50**

NO.2
Chow Mein

NO.2 .... **$17.95**

NO.3
Cold Sesame Noodles

NO.3 .... **$11.50**

NO.4
Cheung Fun

NO.4 .... **$5.25**

Bo ssam

SERVES
6

Koreatown, or K-Town as the small Manhattan enclave is known, blossomed in the 1980s following an influx of immigrants in the 60s and 70s. What it lacked in size (a diminutive few streets compared to Los Angeles' Koreatown), it made up for in dynamism, packed with Korean karaoke and barbecue houses, and wove Korean cuisine into New York's food culture. David Chang's Momofuku was also instrumental and helped champion Korean food around the world.

This crispy pork belly bo ssam is a simpler take on Chang's renowned slow-roasted brown sugar–glazed pork shoulder from Ssam Bar—served with signature scallion and ginger sauce, and bibb lettuce leaves for wrapping.

2 lb 3 oz (1 kg) boneless pork belly, skin scored at ½ in (1 cm) intervals
1 tablespoon fine sea salt
1 tablespoon white sugar
2 teaspoons vegetable oil
2 mixed lettuces, such as bibb (butter) and oak, leaves separated
1 bunch of perilla leaves (optional)
store-bought ssamjang sauce, to serve
steamed jasmine rice and kimchi, to serve

Scallion & ginger sauce

½ bunch of scallions (spring onions), thinly sliced
2 in (5 cm) piece of ginger, finely grated
⅓ cup (80 ml) vegetable oil
1½ tablespoons soy sauce
1½ tablespoons rice wine vinegar
1 teaspoon white sugar

Preheat the oven to 300°F (150°C). Line a baking tray with baking paper.

Scatter the pork flesh with the salt and sugar. Season with pepper. Place on the baking tray, skin-side up, then rub the skin with the vegetable oil.

Roast the pork for 1–1½ hours, until tender. Increase the oven temperature to 465°F (240°C) and roast for a further 20–30 minutes, until the skin is crisp. Remove the pork from the oven and leave to rest for 10 minutes.

Meanwhile, combine the scallion and ginger sauce ingredients in a bowl and set aside until needed.

Thinly slice the pork belly. Arrange on a platter with the scallion and ginger sauce, lettuce and perilla leaves (if using), ssamjang, and steamed rice and kimchi, then invite everyone to make their own Korean wraps.

Night

Jamaican jerk chicken

SERVES
4–6

Home to the largest diaspora of Jamaicans in the United States, New York is well represented with the spicy, multi-faceted flavors from the island, and Caribbean food in general. At some of the best jerk chicken counters, the country's iconic dish tempts devotees and passers-by with its alluring smoky perfume as the chicken develops its signature crisp, blackened skin, while the fragrant marinade keeps the meat tender. The grilled birds are often served chopped into large pieces, on a bed of hearty options, including coconut rice studded with kidney beans (known as "rice and peas").

Douse with bottled tangy barbecue sauce, or mouth-tingling hot sauce if you have some, for a deeply soulful meal.

4 lb 6 oz (2 kg) whole chicken, jointed, or bone-in chicken pieces

Jerk chicken marinade

1 bunch of scallions (spring onions), roughly chopped

1 red onion, quartered

2 habanero chilies, stems removed, deseeded if you like less heat

2 in (5 cm) piece of ginger, chopped

8 garlic cloves, peeled

2 tablespoons thyme leaves

2 tablespoons ground allspice

2 tablespoons soy sauce

2 tablespoons dark brown sugar

1 tablespoon sea salt flakes

1 tablespoon black pepper

⅓ cup (80 ml) vegetable oil

⅓ cup (80 ml) lime juice, plus lime wedges to serve

2 tablespoons apple cider vinegar

Coconut rice & beans

14 oz (400 g) long-grain white rice

2 cups (500 ml) coconut milk

2 scallions (spring onions), finely chopped, plus extra to serve

4 garlic cloves, finely chopped

4 thyme sprigs

2 scotch bonnet or habanero chilies

1 teaspoon ground allspice

14 oz (400 g) tin red kidney beans, rinsed and drained

Place all the jerk chicken marinade ingredients in a food processor and blend to a coarse paste. Transfer to a non-reactive container, add the chicken and turn to coat all over. Cover and marinate in the fridge overnight.

When you're ready to go, preheat a barbecue grill or chargrill plate to medium. Cook the chicken, turning and basting occasionally with the marinade, for 20–25 minutes, until cooked through. Remove from the heat, cover loosely with foil and leave to rest for 5 minutes.

Meanwhile, make the coconut rice and beans. Place all the ingredients, except the kidney beans, in a saucepan. Pour in 2 cups (500 ml) of water, season with salt and pepper and bring to the boil over high heat. Cover with a lid, then reduce the heat to low and cook for 10–15 minutes, until the rice is almost cooked through. Add the beans and cook for a further 5 minutes, or until the rice is tender and the beans are warmed through. Remove from the heat and discard the thyme sprigs and chilies. Using a fork, fluff the rice and beans and season with salt. Scatter with extra scallion.

Serve the jerk chicken with the coconut rice and beans, with lime wedges on the side.

Tacos de adobada

SERVES
4-6

Since the 1990s, New York's Mexican community has ballooned to become one of the largest Latinx populations, along with people from Dominica and Puerto Rico—bringing regional fare to the city, and rivaling Los Angeles and Texas in flavor.

Tacos—particularly the southern Mexican style, comprising soft white corn tortillas and various fillings—are now a mainstay in bodegas, carts, and restaurants across the boroughs. This recipe combines pork with a blend of dried Mexican chilies, spices, and sweet orange (adobada means "marinated" in Spanish), and cooked until tender and almost caramelized. As per tradition, serve with chopped onion and cilantro, lime wedges, salsa, stacks of warm tortillas—and avocado crema for a creamy finish.

◆◆◆

20 corn tortillas, warmed
¼ pineapple, flesh sliced into thin strips, about 1½ in (4 cm) long
½ white onion, finely chopped
1 bunch of cilantro (coriander), leaves finely chopped
lime wedges, to serve

Pork adobada

5 dried guajillo chilies, stems and seeds removed
2 dried ancho chilies, stems and seeds removed
1 onion, chopped
6 garlic cloves, chopped
juice of 1 orange
2 teaspoons smoked paprika
2 teaspoons ground cumin
2 teaspoons ground coriander
2 teaspoons dried oregano
¼ cup (60 ml) apple cider vinegar
1 fresh bay leaf
3 lb 5 oz (1.5 kg) boneless, skinless pork shoulder, cut into ¾ in (2 cm) chunks

Salsa ranchera

6 plum (roma) tomatoes
¼ large onion
1 large garlic clove, peeled
1 fresh jalapeno chili

Avocado crema

2 avocados, roughly chopped
2 tablespoons milk

To make the pork adobada, place the dried chilies and 2 cups (500 ml) of water in a large saucepan over medium–high heat. Bring to the boil, then cook for 5 minutes, or until the chilies have softened. Remove from the heat. Add the onion, garlic, orange juice, paprika, cumin, coriander, oregano, and vinegar and blend with a stick blender until smooth. Add the bay leaf and pork. Bring to the boil, then reduce the heat to medium and cook for 1½ hours, or until the pork is tender. Reduce the heat to medium–low and cook for a further 30–45 minutes, until the liquid has evaporated and the mixture has coated the pork and is starting to caramelize.

Meanwhile, preheat the oven to 430°F (220°C). Place all the salsa ranchera ingredients on a baking tray and roast for 20–25 minutes, until soft and slightly charred. Blend the ingredients in a food processor and season to taste with salt and pepper.

To make the avocado crema, blend the avocado and milk using a stick blender until smooth, adding 1–2 teaspoons extra milk if needed for a nice consistency. Season with salt.

To serve, divide the pork adobada among the warm tacos, dollop with the crema and salsa, top with pineapple and scatter with onion and cilantro. Serve immediately, with lime wedges.

Potato & cheese pierogi

MAKES ABOUT
20

Following waves of migration, Polish and Ukrainian communities bloomed, respectively, in Brooklyn's Greenpoint and a small stretch of East Village now known as Ukrainian Village—and with them, homeland favorite pierogi. These comforting dumplings are stuffed with various fillings, from meat to sauerkraut, and fresh berries with curd, but the most popular is undoubtedly the combination of soft potato, farmers' cheese, caramelized onion, and black pepper. The hand-pleated half-moons are boiled into delicate submission, optionally fried to crisp, then served with buttery onions and sour cream or applesauce.

In the 1970s and 80s, late-night diners serving pierogi fed club-goers by night then babushkas the next day—and the tradition continues in New York today at institutions such as Veselka.

◆◆◆

14 oz (400 g) all-purpose potatoes, peeled, cut into 1¼ in (3 cm) chunks
4½ oz (125 g) butter, chopped
2 large onions, 1 finely chopped, 1 thinly sliced
7 oz (200 g) twarog or cottage cheese
large handful of chopped dill fronds
9 oz (250 g) sour cream

Pierogi dough

1⅔ cups (250 g) all-purpose (plain) flour, plus extra for dusting
½ teaspoon fine sea salt
1 oz (25 g) butter

To make the dough, combine the flour and salt in the bowl of a stand mixer fitted with a dough hook. In a small saucepan, warm the butter and ½ cup (125 ml) of water over medium heat until the butter has melted and the mixture begins to steam (before it comes to the boil). Add the warm mixture to the flour and knead on low speed until combined; add more water, 1 teaspoon at a time, if the mixture is too dry.

Increase the speed and knead the dough for 5 minutes, or until smooth and elastic. Transfer to a bowl, cover with plastic wrap and rest for 1 hour at room temperature.

Place the potato in a saucepan of cold salted water. Bring to the boil over medium–high heat and cook for 12 minutes, or until tender. Drain.

Meanwhile, warm 1½ oz (40 g) of the butter in a frying pan over medium heat. Add the finely chopped onion and season generously with salt and pepper. Cook, stirring, for 10–12 minutes, until soft and caramelized. In a separate pan, melt another 1½ oz (40 g) of the butter over medium heat. Add the sliced onion, season generously with salt and pepper and cook, stirring, for 10–12 minutes, until soft and caramelized. (Alternatively, finely chop all the onion and cook together, using half for the filling and half to serve.)

Continued

Transfer the potato to a large bowl and roughly mash with a fork into ½ in (1 cm) chunks. Add the cheese and the finely chopped caramelized onion. Season generously with salt and pepper and stir to combine. Shape into rough balls of about a tablespoon each; you may need to cool the mixture in the fridge to firm.

Bring a large saucepan of salted water to the boil.

Meanwhile, divide the dough into two even portions and leave one of them covered. Roll the other portion out on a lightly floured work surface until 1/16 in (2 mm) thick. Cut out 10–12 rounds, using a 3¼–4 in (8–10 cm) round cutter. Place a ball of filling in each round and fold the dough over to enclose, pressing the edges to seal and form a crescent shape. Pleat or crimp the edges to ensure there are no holes, or your pierogi will burst during cooking. Transfer to a tray lined with baking paper and repeat with the remaining dough and filling.

Cook half the pierogi in the pan of boiling water for 3 minutes, or until they float to the surface. Transfer with a slotted spoon to a colander. Repeat with the remaining pierogi.

If you'd like to finish your pierogi by pan-frying them, melt the remaining butter in a large frying pan over medium–high heat until hot. Add half the pierogi and cook for 1–2 minutes on each side, until golden and crisp. Transfer to a plate and repeat with the remaining pierogi.

Add the sliced caramelized onion to the pan, give it a stir, then spoon the butter and onion mixture over the pierogi. Season with salt and pepper.

Swirl the dill through the sour cream and serve on the side.

Khachapuri

MAKES
2

Dedicated Georgian restaurants first appeared in migrant enclaves in Brooklyn, then spread throughout Manhattan—driven in large part by khachapuri, the country's addictive, molten cheese-stuffed bread. There are different versions, all salty, soft, and satisfying, but the most famous is khachapuri adjaruli, from the Adjara region bordering the Black Sea, shaped like a boat and sometimes called "cheese boat" for this reason. As the bread bakes, the cheese melts into a golden pool—often topped with egg yolk and butter to enrich, then theatrically swirled to combine. The bread is both a casing and a vehicle for dipping, as well as being endlessly photogenic.

Traditionally, imeruli or sulguni cheese is used. These are difficult to source outside of Georgia, so this recipe uses a blend of mozzarella, ricotta, and feta.

3½ oz (100 g) firm mozzarella, grated
3½ oz (100 g) firm ricotta, crumbled
1¾ oz (50 g) feta, crumbled
2 tablespoons roughly chopped
    parsley leaves
¾ oz (20 g) unsalted butter, melted,
    plus an extra 1½ oz (40 g) butter,
    sliced
2 egg yolks

Khachapuri dough

1½ cups (225 g) bread flour, plus
    extra for dusting
¾ cup (185 ml) lukewarm milk
2 teaspoons olive oil
1 teaspoon dried yeast
1 teaspoon fine sea salt

Place all the dough ingredients in the bowl of a stand mixer fitted with a dough hook. Beat on low speed until combined, then increase the speed to medium–high and knead for 5 minutes, or until smooth and elastic; the dough will be quite wet. Transfer to a greased bowl. Cover and set aside for 1½–2 hours, until doubled in size.

Preheat the oven to 480°F (250°C), or as high as your oven will go. Line a large baking tray with baking paper.

Place the mozzarella, ricotta, feta, and parsley in a bowl. Season with salt and pepper and mix until well combined.

Divide the dough into two even pieces, then roll each piece on a lightly floured work surface into an 8 in (20 cm) round. Transfer to the baking tray and leave to rest for 15 minutes.

Divide the cheese filling between the dough rounds, leaving a 2 in (5 cm) border. Working with one at a time, roll up two sides of the dough to partially enclose the filling, leaving room to hold the egg yolk later on, then press and pinch the ends of the dough together to form two narrow pointed ends, or shape into an oval boat.

Reduce the oven temperature to 430°F (220°C) and bake the khachapuri for 10 minutes. Brush the edges of the bread with the melted butter. Bake for a further 6–8 minutes, until golden and the cheese has melted.

Remove from the oven and use the back of a spoon to make an indent in the filling. Add an egg yolk to each indent and top with the extra butter. Serve immediately, stirring the egg and butter into the cheese mixture. Tear pieces of the bread to dip into the hot cheese.

Night

Pernil with arroz

SERVES
8

With changing economic conditions between 1940 and 1970, large numbers of Puerto Ricans left the countryside for New York, setting up communities in East Harlem—later called Spanish Harlem or El Barrio—and Lower East Side, or Loisaida, a Spanish phonetic pronunciation of the neighborhood. Nuyorican (New York Puerto Rican) culture and the cocina criolla of the island—a cuisine blending indigenous, Spanish, and African influences—took root in the city, and so did some of their most cherished dishes: sancocho, mofongo, and pernil asado with arroz con gandules. The latter, a sumptuous preparation of slow-roasted pork, marinated in sour orange, garlic, and oregano, with pigeon peas dotting glistening rice, is traditional come Christmas and special occasions, and a must-have on restaurant menus.

This recipe is slightly quicker, with boneless pork shoulder, and sofrito-laced rice— but no less satisfying.

5½ lb (2.5 kg) skin-on boneless pork shoulder, skin scored in a cross-hatch, rolled in kitchen string
olive oil, for brushing
1 green bell pepper (capsicum), quartered
6 garlic cloves, peeled
1 onion, roughly chopped
½ bunch of cilantro (coriander) leaves
2 tablespoons oregano leaves
2 tablespoons vegetable oil
1 teaspoon sweet paprika
1 cup (250 g) pureed tomatoes (passata)
3 cups (600 g) medium-grain white rice, rinsed until the water runs clear
5 cups (1.25 litres) chicken stock
3 dried bay leaves
lime wedges and cilantro (coriander) leaves, to serve

Marinade

1 garlic bulb, cloves peeled
½ bunch of cilantro (coriander) leaves
¼ cup fresh oregano leaves
½ cup (125 ml) orange juice
½ cup (125 ml) lime juice
¼ cup (60 ml) olive oil
2 tablespoons sea salt flakes
1 teaspoon black pepper

Place the marinade ingredients in a food processor and blitz together. Transfer the marinade and pork to a snug-fitting plastic container or large zip-lock bag. Turn the pork to coat all over, then marinate in the fridge at least overnight, and up to 3 days.

Remove the pork from the marinade, discarding the marinade. Transfer to an ovenproof Dutch oven (casserole dish), skin side up, and stand for 1 hour to bring to room temperature.

Preheat the oven to 320°F (160°C). Put the lid on the Dutch oven and roast the pork for 2½–3 hours, until tender. Remove the lid, brush the skin of the pork with olive oil and turn the oven up to 400°F (200°C). Roast, uncovered, for a further 30 minutes, or until the skin is golden and crisp.

Blitz the bell pepper, garlic, onion, cilantro, and oregano in a food processor until smooth. Heat the vegetable oil in a saucepan over medium heat. Add the bell pepper sauce and cook, stirring, for 4 minutes, or until slightly thickened. Add the paprika and passata and cook, stirring, for 2 minutes. Add the rice, stock, and bay leaves and stir well to combine. Bring to a simmer, then cook, uncovered, for 12–15 minutes, until the liquid is the level of the rice; there should be little bubbles on the surface of the rice. Cover with a lid, reduce the heat to low and cook for a further 10–15 minutes, until the rice is tender and the liquid is absorbed. Taste and season with salt and pepper.

Remove the pork from the casserole dish and rest for 15 minutes. Cut the skin into bite-sized pieces and shred the meat. Season with salt and pepper. Serve with the rice, lime wedges and cilantro.

Night

Rigatoni alla vodka

SERVES
4

The creamy tomato pasta with a hit of chili and booze, penne alla vodka has many origin stories. None are definitive, but it gained a foothold in America in the 1970s and 80s and now proudly claims a position among the most loved pasta dishes in the country. Deglazing with liquor is common in cookery, but the combination of clean-tasting vodka with sweet, acidic, savory tomatoes heightens the flavors; the alcohol also binds the flavorful cream fat for a glossy, emulsified finish.

In New York, penne alla vodka is a faithful addition to Italian-American menus, and is done with class. The recipe below is inspired by the one served at Carbone's restaurant, with a juicy, oil-slicked Calabrian chili paste imparting more dimension than dried chili flakes, and tossed through rigatoni for more pasta bite.

14 oz (400 g) rigatoni or penne
2 tablespoons extra virgin olive oil
1 large onion, finely chopped
3 garlic cloves, finely chopped
1½ tablespoons Calabrian chili paste
½ cup (125 g) concentrated puree (tomato paste)
½ cup (125 ml) vodka
1 cup (250 ml) pouring cream
¼ teaspoon white sugar
¾ cup (75 g) finely grated parmesan, plus extra to serve

Bring a large saucepan of salted water to the boil. Add the pasta and cook for 2 minutes less than recommended on the packet.

Meanwhile, heat the olive oil in a large deep saucepan over medium heat. Add the onion and cook, stirring, for 5 minutes, or until soft. Season well with salt and pepper, then add the garlic and chili paste and cook, stirring, for 1 minute, or until fragrant.

Add the tomato paste and cook, stirring, for 2 minutes, or until slightly darkened and thickened. Pour in the vodka and cook for 2 minutes, or until reduced slightly. Stir in the cream and sugar and cook for a further 2 minutes, or until well combined.

Drain the pasta, reserving 1 cup (250 ml) of the cooking water. Add the pasta and half the cooking water to the sauce and bring to a simmer, gently tossing the pasta to combine. Add the parmesan and remaining cooking water and cook, tossing gently, until the pasta is al dente and the sauce is just thickened. Remove from the heat and season with salt and pepper.

Divide the pasta among bowls and scatter with extra parmesan to serve.

Night

Mighty brisket platter

SERVES
8

New York may not be a barbecue state like Texas, Tennessee, Alabama, and the Carolinas, but it has developed a rich barbecue subculture, pulling on regional styles from across the country. Pitmasters can be found from Red Hook to Queens in character-filled halls with plenty of room for meat smoking, eating, and drinking, and dishing up pork ribs, sausages, and all the sides on mighty platters. This at-home brisket cheats by cooking a generous fat cap–topped slab in the oven in place of smoking, but celebrates the joys of sticky, crusted, tender beef slathered in traditional smokehouse sauce, served with tangy slaw, buns, and pickles.

◆ ◆ ◆

¼ cup (60 g) dijon mustard
4 lb 6 oz (2 kg) beef brisket with a ¼ in (5 mm) fat cap, trimmed if needed
1½ cups (375 ml) beef stock
8 milk buns, split, warmed
dill pickles, to serve

Dry rub

2 tablespoons sea salt flakes
1 tablespoon freshly cracked black pepper
1 tablespoon brown sugar
2 teaspoons chili powder
1 tablespoon garlic powder
1 tablespoon onion powder
2 teaspoons smoked paprika

Smokehouse sauce

1½ cups (375 g) ketchup
½ cup (125 ml) apple cider vinegar
¼ cup (55 g) brown sugar
¼ cup (60 ml) Worcestershire sauce
1 tablespoon garlic powder
1 tablespoon onion powder
2 teaspoons chili powder

Backyard slaw

⅓ cup (90 g) sour cream
2 tablespoons whole-egg mayonnaise
⅓ cup (80 ml) apple cider vinegar
2 teaspoons dijon mustard
10½ oz (300 g) finely shredded white and red cabbage
10½ oz (300 g) finely shredded carrot

Preheat the oven to 265°F (130°C).

Combine the dry rub spices in a small bowl. Spread the mustard all over the brisket and place in a large roasting tin. Scatter half the dry rub over the flesh sides of the brisket. Turn the brisket so the fat cap is facing upwards and scatter with the remaining dry rub. Pour the beef stock into the roasting tin, taking care not to drizzle it over the brisket. Cover the pan tightly with foil. Cook the brisket for 5–6 hours, until fork tender.

Meanwhile, place all the smokehouse sauce ingredients in a saucepan over medium heat. Bring to a simmer, stirring occasionally, then remove from the heat. Set aside until needed.

To make the slaw, combine the sour cream, mayonnaise, vinegar, and mustard in a large bowl and season with salt and pepper. Add the mixed cabbage and carrot, and toss to combine. Cover and refrigerate until ready to serve.

Increase the oven temperature to 480°F (250°C), or as high as your oven will go. Remove the foil from the roasting tin. Roast the brisket for a further 10 minutes, or until the top looks like it's almost bubbling and is slightly crusted.

Carefully remove the brisket from the tin, taking care to keep the top intact. Discard the drippings. Carve the meat across the grain into ½–¾ in (1–2 cm) thick slices.

Serve the brisket with the slaw, buns, pickles and smokehouse sauce for dipping.

Veal parm

SERVES
2-4

The "parm", as it is lovingly abbreviated, is closely related to Italian parmigiana, but the two are not the same. Eggplant (aubergine) alla parmigiana is a lighter affair, born in Southern Italy around the 18th century—while the heftier adaptation, coated in breadcrumbs and topped with a thick jacket of cheese, came to life in America with Italian immigrants whose new livelihoods now allowed for the price of meat.

Eschewing delicacy for decadence, parms today are a truly satisfying and almost spiritual experience for New Yorkers, the bright, tart sauce the perfect foil for crisp, crumbed meat and bubbling mozzarella and parmesan—especially in the cooler months paired with buttered or sauced pasta, or stuffed into a hero roll. Eggplant, chicken, and veal are the most beloved parms here—and veal the luxurious choice at the city's Italian-American institutions and hotspots.

2 × 10½ oz (300 g) veal rib-eye steaks, on the bone
1½ cups (90 g) panko breadcrumbs
2½ teaspoons fennel seeds, toasted, crushed
1 cup (100 g) finely grated parmesan
⅔ cup (100 g) all-purpose (plain) flour
1 egg
¼ cup (60 ml) milk
2 garlic cloves, crushed
olive oil, for shallow-frying and drizzling
7 oz (200 g) buffalo or fresh mozzarella, thinly sliced

Rich tomato sugo

1 oz (30 g) butter
½ onion, finely chopped
2 garlic cloves, finely chopped
¼ teaspoon chili flakes
¼ cup (60 ml) white wine
14 oz (400 g) pureed tomatoes (passata)
½ teaspoon white sugar

To make the tomato sugo, melt the butter in a saucepan over medium heat. Add the onion and garlic, season with salt and pepper and cook, stirring, for 5 minutes, or until soft. Add the chili flakes and stir for about 1 minute, until fragrant. Splash in the wine, increase the heat and bring to the boil for 1 minute. Add the pureed tomatoes and sugar, then reduce the heat to medium and cook, stirring occasionally, for 10–12 minutes to develop the flavor. Remove from the heat, season with salt and pepper and cover to keep warm.

Preheat the oven broiler (grill) to high. Line a baking tray with baking paper.

Cut the flesh of the veal steaks horizontally through the middle but don't slice all the way through. Open up the steaks to butterfly them, keeping the meat attached to the bone. Using a meat mallet or rolling pin, pound the veal until both steaks are ¼ in (5 mm) thick. Season generously with salt and pepper.

Combine the panko breadcrumbs, fennel seeds, and half the parmesan in a shallow bowl. Place the flour in another shallow bowl. Whisk the egg, milk, and garlic in a third shallow bowl to combine and season with salt and pepper.

Dust the flattened veal in the flour, shaking off the excess, then dip in the egg mixture. Finally, coat in the panko breadcrumbs, pressing until well coated all over.

Continued

Fill a large deep frying pan with ½ in (1.5 cm) of olive oil and heat over medium–high heat until shimmering. Cook one crumbed veal steak for 2 minutes on each side, or until golden and crisp (it won't be cooked through). Transfer to a wire rack set over a baking tray. Repeat with the remaining crumbed veal.

Transfer the fried veal to the prepared tray. Top each portion with a few spoonfuls of sugo, leaving some areas exposed for crispness and crunch. Top with the mozzarella slices, then scatter all over with two-thirds of the remaining parmesan. Drizzle with olive oil.

Broil (grill) for 3–4 minutes, until the cheese is bubbling and light golden. Transfer to warmed serving plates, season with pepper and serve with any remaining sugo and the parmesan.

NY pizza by the slice (two ways)

MAKES
2 PIZZAS

◆◆◆

You could write a whole book on New York's most iconic of dishes. At the end of the 19th century, hundreds of thousands of Italian migrants moved to New York, and with them came tomato-topped Southern Italian pizzas. Gennaro Lombardi, on Spring Street in Little Italy, opened a restaurant with a coal-fired oven and started selling whole pies by the slice—two innovations to feed hungry, time-poor, and cash-strapped factory workers, and both unheard of in the homeland. Following World War II, returned veterans with a taste for Italian flavors fueled pizza's spread around the country—and by that time, almost every street corner in New York had pizza by the slice.

In 2008, 2 Bros. Pizza started selling pizza slices for $1 to outprice the standard $2 subway fare, and competitors soon sprouted throughout the city, giving rise to the 'dollar slice'—a not good, but perfectly acceptable, student and drunk alternative to the artisan slices found everywhere else.

New York pizza is characterized by a medium-thin, lightly crisped and chewy crust—a sturdy structure to support a wide-cut slice that droops slightly at the tip and can be folded in half to eat. Glass cabinets display a range of toppings. The best loved are still the classics, including tomato-sauced pepperoni and white slice—here with ricotta, mozzarella, and lemon.

Pizza dough

2⅔ cups (400 g) bread flour, plus
  extra for dusting
1 cup (250 ml) water, at room
  temperature
1 teaspoon dried yeast
2 teaspoons fine sea salt
2 teaspoons superfine (caster) sugar
1 tablespoon olive oil

Pepperoni slice

1 oz (25 g) butter
1 tablespoon olive oil
½ onion, finely chopped
1 garlic clove, finely chopped
1 teaspoon dried oregano
pinch of chili flakes, plus extra
  to serve (optional)
14 oz (400 g) tin whole plum (roma)
  tomatoes
1 large basil sprig
6½ oz (180 g) firm mozzarella, grated
3½ oz (100 g) pepperoni, sliced

White slice

¼ cup (60 ml) pouring cream
6½ oz (180 g) firm mozzarella, grated
7 oz (200 g) ricotta
1 oz (30 g) pecorino romano,
  finely grated
1 lemon, zested, then cut into wedges

Place the pizza dough ingredients in the bowl of a stand mixer fitted with a dough hook. Knead for 1–2 minutes, until combined. Stand for 15 minutes to rest the gluten, then knead for a further 7 minutes, or until smooth and elastic. Transfer to a greased bowl, cover and refrigerate for 24–48 hours to cold ferment.

Remove the dough from the fridge 2 hours before using.

Meanwhile, to make the red sauce for the pepperoni slice pizza, warm the butter and oil in a saucepan over medium heat. Cook the onion and garlic, stirring frequently, for 6–7 minutes, until soft and starting to caramelize. Add the oregano and chili flakes and stir for 1 minute. Add the tomatoes, crushing them with a fork, then add the basil sprig. Cook, stirring occasionally, for 15 minutes to develop the flavor. Remove from the heat, discard the basil sprig and blend with a stick blender until mostly smooth but with some chunkiness.

Preheat the oven to 500°F (260°C) or as high as your oven will go.

Divide the dough into two even balls. Roll one dough ball out on a lightly floured work surface. Gently press the dough into a rough 8 in (20 cm) circle, leaving the outer edge thicker than the center to form a rim. Gently stretch the dough by draping it over your knuckles to form a 12–13½ in (30–34 cm) circle, about ¼ in (5 mm) thick. Transfer to a 12 in (30 cm) round metal pizza tray.

For the pepperoni slice pizza, spread ½ cup (125 ml) of the red sauce over the dough, leaving a border (reserve the remaining sauce for another use). Scatter with the mozzarella and top with the pepperoni.

Bake the pizza for 12–15 minutes, until the cheese has melted with some browned spots, and the crust is golden brown and puffed. Transfer to a cutting board and leave to stand for 5 minutes. Scatter with more chili flakes, if desired, and cut into slices to serve.

For the white slice pizza, roll out the remaining dough ball in the same way and transfer to the pizza tray. Spread the cream over the dough, then scatter with the mozzarella. Dollop the ricotta all around, then scatter with the pecorino. Bake and leave to stand as directed above. Sprinkle with the lemon zest, cut into slices and serve with the lemon wedges.

Above NY pizza by the slice (two ways) 224

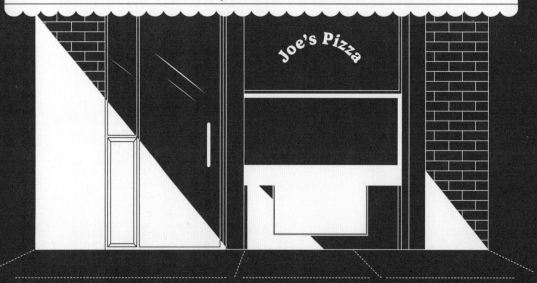

7 CARMINE STREET, NEW YORK,
NY 10014

The Quintessential
New York slice

Joe Pozzuoli Jr

M y father, Joe Pozzuoli Sr, emigrated to America in 1956 from the Italian city of Caserta, just a few miles from Naples, widely considered the birthplace of pizza.

We lived in a lively Italian-American enclave in Brooklyn, where children played unsupervised in the street, and you could smell the aroma of strong Italian coffee coming from your neighbor's kitchen window in the morning, and fresh tomato sauce slowly cooking in the evening.

He started Joe's Pizza in 1975, serving a classic Neapolitan-style New York slice. He chose Greenwich Village because of its bohemian vibe at the time. The neighborhood had a lot of character, and it was fun feeding musicians and artists, as well as the local residents. It was a truly unique and vibrant community. We were always open until the wee hours of the morning. Whenever you were hungry, Joe's was there for you.

A small independent pizza shop is a lot of hard work with grueling hours—it's not a 9–5 job. Our pizza is a nuanced, handmade product and quality control is key. At first, Joe Sr had only his children for staff. Today, it has expanded to a rare still-family-owned business with multiple generations—children, grandchildren and cousins—still actively involved in the business.

Pizza was first introduced in the US northeast where it quickly became popular, and some of the oldest pizza restaurants can be found here. A small group of Italian immigrants started making this little hometown dish out of necessity, but also out of passion. A simple meal made of just bread, tomatoes and cheese was a part of home, their comfort food. Eventually, the local corner pizza shop became a spot where everyone could get an affordable bite, quickly.

Joe's has seen so many characters over the years. There was a young 95 lb (43 kg) woman, who came in every week to devour a full 20" (50 cm) pizza all in one sitting. We still don't know how this was even physically possible. There was a 97-year-old Italian immigrant who would come in every morning, lay down 10 cents and have 'una Coca Cola' and nothing else—we never told her the soda was actually 75 cents. We've served countless musicians and artists on their way up, during their lean years when they couldn't afford much more than a slice of pizza for their meal. And we've had endless Saturday nights where the crowds from nearby bars all congregate at Joe's until the intersection is blocked and the police have to move everyone on. We've even had customers propose marriage, because they met while waiting in line for pizza.

At our original location, dough is made, mixed, and cut every morning and every evening. On a busy day, we easily sell 300–400 large pizzas.

We are busiest during the lunch rush, but we can also be quite busy between 1 am and 3 am, when people come in for a late-night snack to end their night.

A perfect New York pizza is a thin crispy crust, just the right amount of sauce and cheese, totally foldable without breaking—and served just hot enough to not burn the roof of your mouth. Ours is still the same recipe as in 1975. We sell mostly plain cheese, but pepperoni is still our best-selling topping.

New York has often been called the capital of the world and I think it still deserves that title. It's a truly global community with people from all walks of life. We're very happy that Joe's Pizza is a part of the special tapestry of NYC, and we are proud to be the 'quintessential New York slice'.

EST. 1975

JOE'S PIZZA

Fresh!

CALL NOW
212-366-1182

MENU

PIES

CLASSIC CHEESE PIE
8 SLICES $24

ADD ANY ONE TOPPING $28

FRESH MOZZARELLA PIE
8 SLICES $28

SICILIAN SQUARE PIE
8 SLICES $28

TOPPINGS

PEPPERONI, SAUSAGE,
MEATBALL $12

PEPPERS, ONION, BROCCOLI,
MUSHROOM, BLACK OLIVES $3

GARLIC, EXTRA CHEESE $2

DRINKS

SNAPPLE $2.50

IMPORTED COKE $3.50

FANTA $3.50

SPRITE $3.50

Late-night samosa chaat

SERVES
4

At night and into the early hours of the morning, Indian delis and small storefronts welcome taxi drivers through to college students with a comforting and affordable array of curries and chaat (Indian snacks). Quick to assemble and devour, chaat also revive the weary with their delicious combo of crunchy, spicy, tangy, and sweet notes. The pick of choice is samosa chaat: a smashed potato samosa covered in fragrant chana masala (garbanzo bean curry), creamy dahi (yoghurt), and sweet and sour cilantro and tamarind chutneys, with chopped onion and crunchy sev (fried noodles) for layers of texture and crunch.

This quicker version uses tinned garbanzo beans in the curry, as well as store-bought samosas, with deeply satisfying results.

2 tablespoons ghee or vegetable oil
1 onion, finely chopped
4 garlic cloves, finely chopped
1½ in (4 cm) piece of ginger, finely grated
1 long green chili, finely chopped
2 teaspoons ground coriander
2 teaspoons ground cumin
½ teaspoon ground turmeric
¼ teaspoon ground chili
14 oz (400 g) tomatoes, finely chopped
2 × 14 oz (400 g) tins garbanzo beans (chickpeas), drained and rinsed
1 teaspoon garam masala
8 store-bought samosas, warmed until crisp
1 cup (250 g) plain yoghurt, whisked with ¼ cup (60 ml) of water until smooth
70 g (¼ cup) tamarind chutney (or a combination of cilantro/coriander and mint chutneys and other chutneys)
½ red onion, finely chopped
½ bunch of cilantro (coriander), leaves finely chopped
sev (fried noodles), to serve (optional)

Heat the ghee in a saucepan over medium heat. Add the onion, season with salt and pepper and cook, stirring, for 10 minutes, or until soft and starting to brown.

Add the garlic, ginger, and chopped chili and cook, stirring, for 1 minute, or until softened. Add the coriander, cumin, turmeric, and ground chili and stir for another minute, or until fragrant.

Stir in the tomatoes and cook for 2 minutes, or until softened, scraping the base of the pan to ensure nothing sticks. Add the garbanzo beans and 2 cups (500 ml) of water and season with salt and pepper. Bring to the boil, then reduce the heat to medium–low. Cover and cook for 30 minutes, or until the garbanzo beans have softened and the flavors have developed. Using a wooden spoon, break up some of the garbanzo beans to thicken the broth. Remove from the heat, sprinkle with the garam masala and season with salt and pepper.

To serve, divide the chana masala among four bowls. Break the samosas and place on top. Drizzle with the yoghurt and chutneys, then scatter with the red onion and cilantro, and sev, if desired. Enjoy straight away.

Steakhouse porterhouse

SERVES
2-4

Enjoying a good steak has long been a New York tradition, and it has always been an event. It began with beefsteak in the mid-19th century, when men would congregate in halls and unceremoniously consume trays of meat and pitchers of beer together. With the women's vote, it took on a more sophisticated tenor and the New York steakhouse was eventually born.

Today, to visit a steakhouse is to experience old-world New York, with hallowed rooms and classic pairings of shrimp cocktails to start, sides of creamed spinach and twice-cooked potato, and New York cheesecake to finish, with these being still among the best meals in the city. There's also a modern refinement, with perfectly cooked prime cuts of meat in generous portions for sharing to rival any in the world.

Most steakhouses dry-age their cuts, from porterhouse to New York strip, adding depth of flavor and tenderizing the meat. The secret for cooking at home is refrigerating the steak uncovered overnight, or setting it aside at room temperature while it de-chills, as well as basting with butter as it cooks.

Cut the meat and arrange around the bone on warm plates for the full New York moment.

2 × 12½–14 oz (350–400 g) bone-in porterhouse or T-bone steaks
1 tablespoon olive oil
sea salt flakes and freshly cracked black pepper
2½ oz (75 g) butter, melted
lemon cheeks, to serve

Creamed spinach

10½ oz (300 g) baby spinach
¾ oz (20 g) butter
1 small onion, finely chopped
2 garlic cloves, finely chopped
1½ tablespoons all-purpose (plain) flour
½ cup (125 ml) milk
½ cup (125 ml) pouring cream
pinch of freshly grated nutmeg
½ cup (50 g) grated parmesan (optional)

Remove the steaks from the fridge and set aside, uncovered, for 30 minutes before cooking, to come to room temperature.

To make the creamed spinach, place the spinach in a colander in the sink and pour boiling water over to wilt the leaves (you may need to do this twice). Leave to cool slightly, then squeeze to remove the excess water.

Melt the butter in a saucepan over medium heat. Cook the onion and garlic, stirring, for 5 minutes, or until soft. Add the flour and cook for 1 minute, or until golden. Gradually add the milk and cook, stirring, until thickened. Add the spinach, cream, nutmeg, and parmesan (if using) and stir until melted and combined. Season with salt and pepper. Remove from the heat and keep warm.

Warm your serving plates. Heat the olive oil in a large cast-iron skillet or heavy-based frying pan over high heat until very hot and smoking. Meanwhile, lightly pat the steaks dry with paper towel. Season the steaks generously with sea salt flakes and freshly cracked black pepper.

Continued

→

Night

Cook the steaks for 2 minutes without touching them, for a thick crust to develop. (If the steaks don't fit in the pan with space between them, cook them separately to ensure each one cooks properly.)

Turn the steaks over and add the butter to the pan. Cook for a further 2 minutes for medium-rare, spooning the melted butter over the top during cooking.

Transfer the steaks to the warm serving plates and drizzle with most of the butter. Cover each one with another plate and stand for 3–5 minutes to rest.

Slice the steaks from the bone, cut into 1¼ in (3 cm) thick pieces and arrange back into the shape of the steaks. Drizzle the remaining buttery sauce over the top and serve with the creamed spinach and lemon cheeks.

I ♥ NY cheesecake

SERVES
12

Cheesecake certainly wasn't invented in New York, but the style now synonymous with the city is famous the world over. Accounts trace the New York cheesecake back to the early 20th century, when curd cheese was replaced with sour cream and newly mass-produced cream cheese (also out of New York State), giving it the smooth, silky texture and rich, just-tangy flavor it's now beloved for.

You can still find it made the way it was a century ago alongside newer takes at bakeries, delis and steakhouses across the city. The art is in taking the time to cook it delicately, with room-temperature cream cheese to avoid lumps, and a water bath for a just-set finish. A touch of cinnamon adds a wonderful fragrant note to the base.

2 lb 3 oz (1 kg) cream cheese,
   at room temperature
1⅓ cups (295 g) superfine
   (caster) sugar
1 tablespoon natural vanilla extract
4 eggs
10½ oz (300 g) sour cream

Cheesecake crust

7 oz (200 g) graham crackers
   or digestive biscuits
¼ cup (55 g) superfine (caster) sugar
½ teaspoon ground cinnamon
pinch of fine sea salt
3 oz (90 g) unsalted butter, melted

Preheat the oven to 350°F (180°C). Grease an 8¾ in (22 cm) springform cake tin and line the base with baking paper. Wrap the outside base with a double layer of foil—make sure it's tight!

To make the cheesecake crust, blend the crackers in a food processor until finely ground, then add the sugar, cinnamon, and salt and blend to combine. Add the butter and process until well moistened, then tip the mixture into the cake tin. Using the base of a glass, press the crumbs down to make a firm base. Bake the crust for 15 minutes, or until golden.

Meanwhile, using electric beaters, beat the cream cheese in a large bowl until very smooth. Add the sugar and vanilla extract and beat for 2 minutes, or until well combined. Add the eggs, one at a time, beating until well combined after each addition. Add the sour cream and beat for another minute. Scrape the base of the bowl to ensure there are no lumps, beating to combine if necessary.

Turn the oven down to 320°F (160°C). Pour the cheesecake filling over the crust, then place the cake tin in a larger baking dish. Pour boiling water into the baking dish, until it reaches halfway up the cake tin. Carefully transfer the baking dish to the oven. Bake the cheesecake for 1 hour, or until set on the top and around the edge; it will still have a wobble in the center.

Turn the oven off and rest the cheesecake in the oven with the door closed for 1 hour.

Remove the cake tin from the water bath and place on a wire rack. Leave to cool to room temperature. Cover with plastic wrap and chill in the fridge for at least a few hours, or overnight, until the filling is completely cool and silky.

ABOUT
THE AUTHOR

Yasmin Newman is an Australian-Filipina food and travel writer, and culinary director. She is the author of four cookbooks: *7000 Islands*, *The Desserts of New York*, *Under Coconut Skies* and *EAT NYC*.

She is also the host of television series *A Taste of the Philippines*. She currently lives in Sydney, Australia, with her husband and two children.

Thank You!

YOUR PATRONAGE IS APPRECIATED

TABLE	NO. PERSONS	WATER	AMOUNT OF CHECK

L ike all my books, this was a labor of love and would not have been possible without the help of countless people.

First and foremost, my brother Terry and his wife, Krista, who live in New York and fostered my love for the city. Over the many years, they've housed my family and me for extended periods of time in their East Village apartment, and shown us the heart and soul of the city. For *EAT NYC*, they were by my side at every step, from zigzagging across the boroughs to trying different restaurants, to taste-testing all the dishes. Sharing the adventure with family to write this book made it all the more joyful.

Writing, however, is only one step of the process. Thank you Smith Street Books for bringing this book to life! Among the many truly talented people are my publisher, Paul McNally, for his ongoing belief in me and his big ideas;

my managing editor, Lucy Heaver, for her impeccable sensibilities; photographer Alan Benson for his stunning lifestyle and food shots, stylist Lucy Tweed for her masterful touch and Emi Chiba at Evi-O Studio for the gorgeous design. Plus Sarah Mayoh, Jaimee Curdie, Katri Hilden and more!

Thank you, as always, to my husband, Steve, and children, Inès and Alejo, for bearing with me as I wrote this book.

And lastly, thank you to all the New Yorkers I met along the way, especially the food innovators, and those who make this city one of a kind.

TAX

Index

Index

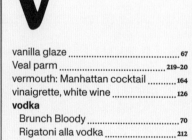

Published in 2024 by Smith Street Books
Naarm (Melbourne) | Australia
smithstreetbooks.com

ISBN: 978-1-9227-5423-3

Smith Street Books respectfully acknowledges the Wurundjeri People of the Kulin Nation, who are the Traditional Owners of the land on which we work, and we pay our respects to their Elders past and present.

Publishing director: Paul McNally
Managing editor: Lucy Heaver
Editor: Katri Hilden
Design and illustrations: Evi-O. Studio | Emi Chiba, Siena Zadro
Typesetter: Megan Ellis
Photography: Alan Benson
Food styling: Lucy Tweed
Food preparation: Sarah Mayoh and Jaimee Curdie
Proofreader: Pamela Dunne
Indexer: Helena Holmgren

Printed & bound in China by C&C Offset Printing Co., Ltd.

Book 336
10 9 8 7 6 5 4 3 2